P9-DUS-492

FIELDING'S THEORY OF THE NOVEL

FIELDING'S THEORY OF THE NOVEL

BY

FREDERICK OLDS BISSELL, Jr., Ph.D.

Instructor in English, Cornell University

NEW YORK

COOPER SQUARE PUBLISHERS, INC.

1969

Originally Published 1933
Published by Cooper Square Publishers, Inc.
59 Fourth Avenue, New York, N. Y. 10003
Library of Congress Catalog Card No. 68-57713

Printed in the United States of America

PREFACE

This study is a complete revision of a doctoral dissertation prepared some three years ago under the guidance of Professor Frederick C. Prescott. It attempts to describe the chief sources of Fielding's theory of the novel, to present and interpret that theory, and to show its application in *Joseph Andrews* and *Tom Jones*. The chapter on the sources of Fielding's theory is largely a synthesis of critical opinion on the various types of literature considered. I am particularly indebted to Frank W. Chandler's *The Literature of Roguery* for the material on the picaresque genre; to Edward C. Baldwin's monograph on *The Character Books of the Seventeenth Century, in Relation to the Development of the Novel* for the discussion of that topic; to Ashley H. Thorndike's *English Comedy* for the section on the comedy of manners; to Austin Dobson's essay on Fielding's Library for the remarks on Fielding's classical reading; and to Wilbur L. Cross's *The Development of the English Novel* for various critical points.

I wish to thank Professor Prescott for the advice and encouragement which he has kindly given me during all stages of this work and Professor Clark S. Northup for editing the manuscript and reading the proofs.

F. O. B., Jr.

Cornell University,
February 4, 1933.

CONTENTS

FIELDING'S THEORY OF THE NOVEL

FIELDING'S THEORY OF THE NOVEL

I

THE SOURCES OF FIELDING'S THEORY

THE THEORY of the novel stated and practiced by Fielding was mainly the natural outgrowth of realistic influences which had been affecting English prose fiction for nearly two centuries. These influences, in the beginning, came from southern Europe, especially from Spain. The direct line in the development of English fiction was broken in the first half of the sixteenth century, and when, midway in the reign of Elizabeth, creative work began anew, the main impetus came from the importation of the romances of chivalry, typified by *Amadis de Gaule*, and of the picaresque novels, the first of which was *Lazarillo de Tormes*. The tendency of the romance of chivalry was always toward the fantastic; it represented life in the setting of strange, improbable, or impossible adventures, or idealized the virtues and the vices of human nature. The picaresque novel, on the other hand, tended to deal realistically with actual life. In between these two forms came the burlesque romance, first and best exemplified by *Don Quixote*. To the picaresque novel and the burlesque romance Fielding owes much of his conception of the novel. His novels are realistic, like the picaresque novels, and satirical, like the burlesque romances.

To later forms in English literature Fielding is also indebted for parts of his theory. The character sketch of the seventeenth century and the essays of Addison and Steele in *The Spectator* furnished him with valuable methods and materials for his delineations of human character. The comedy of manners as developed by Etherege, Wycherley, and Congreve, and as imitated by himself, taught him to use principles of dramatic construction, to reproduce conversation vividly, and to satirize human frailties. Lastly, to his wide reading of the Greek and Latin classics and their critics Fielding owes his theory of the comic epic.

For the picaresque element in Fielding's theory we must turn to the picaresque genre. As Frank W. Chandler says in *The Literature of Roguery*, "the true test of the genre is roguery's preponderance . . . the test of form, though more precise, is less generally applicable."[1] The picaresque novel is the most notable type of the literature of roguery. As conceived in Spain and matured in France, the picaresque novel is the fictitious comic biography (or more often the autobiography) of an anti-hero who makes his way in the world through the service of masters, sometimes satirizing their personal faults, as well as their trades and professions. It possesses, therefore, two features of interest: one, the rogue and his tricks; the other, less important, the manners he satirizes. Since the rogue moves from master to master, he is often a traveler; but we must not confuse the picaresque novel with the novel of mere adventure.

The close relationship between the picaresque novel and the burlesque romance of chivalry is seen in *Don Quixote*, which is primarily a burlesque romance, though akin to the picaresque novel. The picaresque novel is an indirect attack on the romance of chivalry, realistic, cynical in tone, and glorifying the vulgar rogue instead of the idealized, saintly knight. *Don Quixote* is a direct attack on the romance of chivalry, meant to demolish the entire mischievous pile of romantic absurdity by placing the world of romance in the real world and letting the characters and sentiments of each mutually play upon one another. The result is that the knight is treated like a madman and his squire is tossed in a blanket. Thus, Cervantes uses the realism of the picaresque novel to expose the absurdity of the romance of chivalry.

Don Quixote, besides marking an epoch in the history of realism, contains, combined with pathos, a new quality of humor, with sparkle and kindly feeling instead of hard picaresque cynicism. Under the sway of this Quixotic humor are Fielding,

[1] F. W. Chandler, *The Literature of Roguery*, p.5.

Goldsmith, Sterne, Thackeray, and in a less degree, Smollett, Scott, Dickens, and Bulwer. In them we find a long list of Quixotic characters, including Parson Adams, Uncle Toby, Jonathan Oldbuck, and Colonel Newcome.

In France the burlesque romance and picaresque novel flourished in the seventeenth and eighteenth centuries as popular literature in reaction to the romance of chivalry. The *Roman Comique* (1651-57) of Paul Scarron, perhaps the best of the French burlesque romances, was indebted to the Spanish picaresque novel for its plan, spirit, and episodes. It mingled romance with realism, abandoned the original picaresque form, substituted farcical scenes and tricks for sordid cheating, and narrowed the range of society observed. Scarron exercised considerable influence upon the English novelists of the eighteenth century, particularly upon Smollett. Fielding imitated Scarron's facetious manner of beginning and ending his chapters. The farcical scenes in *Joseph Andrews*, such as Adams's and Trulliber's pigsty conference, Adams's encounter with the pan of hog's blood and the tub of water, or the mistakes by night at Booby Hall, also recall Scarron.

Le Roman Bourgeois (1666) of Antoine Furetière was burlesque only in part. The taste for travesty of the romances was at this time already in decline and middle-class realism was tending to displace the extravagant as well as the roguish. The scandalous intrigues in bourgeois life, borrowed from the Spanish picaresque stories, were, however, retained. *Le Roman Bourgeois* is noteworthy as the most graphic account of the ways of the bourgeoisie that had yet appeared in fiction.

Lesage's *Gil Blas* (1715, 1724, 1735) first fully realized the possibilities of the romance of roguery. It resembled the Spanish picaresque stories in the adventurous career of its anti-hero, his shifts of condition through the service of various masters, his satire at their expense, his progress from poverty to a competence, his survey of actual manners, and the looseness of his story, with its interpolated biographies and lack of organic unity. It differed from these in its choice of an anti-hero from respectable middle-class life, in minimizing his roguery, awakening his conscience, and softening his heart. "In short, *Gil Blas* outdid the Spanish picaresque tales in art, morality, humanity, and breadth of appeal. It raised to the highest power their merits, and eliminated so far as possible their defects."[1] In *Gil Blas* the picaresque type had attained such perfection that thereafter its decline or complete transformation could alone be expected. *Gil Blas* was the great distributor of the picaresque influence, which deeply affected eighteenth century English fiction.

We may safely assume that Fielding had read these books and that undoubtedly they assisted in forming his theory of the novel. The realism of his novels, dealing, as it largely does, with lower and middle-class life, the nature of his plots, with their peripatetic and episodic adventures, his satirical method in *Joseph Andrews* and *Tom Jones*, are clearly legacies in part from the picaresque and burlesque traditions.

Fielding's affinity with Cervantes appears first of all in his keen perception of the ridiculous in character and action. His debt to Cervantes for the character of Parson Adams is considerable. Secondly, both affect a certain drollery in style, which frequently takes a mock-heroic turn. Thirdly, both study the characters of certain lower classes of men and women: innkeepers, hostlers, chambermaids, puppet-show men, and so forth. Fourthly, both have a refreshing geniality of temperament; and finally, both group their chapters into books, give humorous or satiric descriptions of the contents of their chapters, and introduce extraneous stories or episodes into their narratives.

But Fielding, in saying that *Joseph Andrews* is "written in the manner of Cervantes," overestimated his debt to the Spaniard. In the essentials of its greatness the kind of novel Fielding created owed little to the genius of Cervantes. It has not the air of romance, the aspiration after imaginary good, the vague longing after something more of *Don Quixote*. Then too, each of Cervantes's leading characters has a kind of abnormal individuality of his own; as Hazlitt says, they do not so much belong to a class as form a

[1] F. W. Chandler, *The Literature of Roguery*, vol. 1, p.23.

class by themselves. Fielding set out to picture the ordinary life of his time, to give faithful pictures of men and women in ordinary walks of life. He had little use for the abnormal, the grotesque, or the unnatural; his own experiences supplied him with sufficient material for the purposes of his art.

The several resemblances to the picaresque novel in Fielding's work appear most strikingly in *Joseph Andrews*. It is an epic of the road; the characters are mainly those of the picaresque novel of Spain or France, and the plot is neither skilful nor elaborate. In these respects and in the mock-heroic descriptions it contains, *Joseph Andrews* resembles novels like *Le Roman Comique* or *Gil Blas*. There is no evidence that *Joseph Andrews* is a direct imitation of these novels, but as his references to them[1] might indicate, Fielding probably had them in mind.

Fielding's most considerable debt for *Joseph Andrews* is to Marivaux, not to his *Marianne*, but to *Le Paysan Parvenu* (1735, 1736),[2] which, like Prévost's *Manon Lescaut*, departs from the picaresque tradition by portraying low life more sentimentally, like the novels of Richardson. *Le Paysan Parvenu* was a recent publication when Fielding wrote *Joseph Andrews*. He refers often to Marivaux and knew his writings well. There are several resemblances between the two novels in characters and episodes. Fielding's hero, Joseph, like Marivaux's hero, Jacob, is a young servant whose beauty and charm make his mistress and other women fall in love with him. Lady Booby resembles Jacob's mistress as Marivaux describes her. Sir Thomas Booby and his lady, like Jacob's master and mistress, are far from affectionate. Betty, the chambermaid, like Marivaux's Genevieve, succumbs to the hero's charms, and also receives the attentions of her master. The greatest resemblance, however, is in the account of Lady Booby's infatuation for the hero and her interviews with him. In Marivaux's novel Jacob behaves very differently from Joseph. Fielding's purpose of burlesquing *Pamela* forced him to make Joseph differ from Jacob by being virtuous in this incident.

[1] *Joseph Andrews*, Book III, Chapter I.

[2] H. K. Banerji, *Henry Fielding, His Life and Works*, p.113.

Jacob's affair with his mistress may also have suggested Tom Jones's liaison with Lady Bellaston in the later novel.

The influence of the Spanish and French picaresque novel and burlesque romance on *Tom Jones* and *Amelia*, except for the general features already discussed, is not discernible in any particulars. In both novels we find Fielding's powers in their maturity and discover no considerable direct borrowing from other writers. The general resemblances indicated, however, help to establish the point that Fielding's theory of the novel was drawn partly from these sources.

The first important English picaresque fiction was Nash's *The Unfortunate Traveler* (1594), which was also the last of any literary merit for over a century.[1] It combined adventure with artistic realism, but these qualities disappeared during the seventeenth century. During this period the old romances of chivalry, such as *Amadis de Gaule* and *Le Grand Cyrus*, were revived and regained their popularity. Such picaresque works of the time as Kirkman and Head's *The English Rogue*, while realistic, are devoid of anything like unified structure and literary quality. *The English Rogue* reveals the tendency of English picaresque fiction during the Restoration to forsake direct observation and revert to the type of the old jestbooks and fabliaux, in sifting unrelated tricks and rogue stories out of foreign fiction. The romance of roguery languished, to be revived in the second decade of the eighteenth century by two forces: the naturalism and character-drawing of Defoe, and the literary inspiration of Lesage.[2]

Defoe borrowed from the picaresque novel only the observational method. "The jests and fabliaux, the tricks of the Italian novella or the Spanish romance of roguery count for little in the modern novel, and the first to turn his back on them is Defoe."[3] Defoe, with Lesage, was the first to endow the picaresque form with a unity deeper than the anti-hero's character. He surpasses

[1] F. W. Chandler, *The Literature of Roguery*, vol. 1, p.193.

[2] F. W. Chandler, *op. cit.*, vol. 1, p.229.

[3] Id. p.286.

Lesage in adhering to the unity of character; his primary aim is to portray character, though he has little perception of delicate shades of behavior, or of the change and development of character through experience. In *Moll Flanders* and *Colonel Jack* Defoe sounds the note of the modern novel in subordinating incident to character and in considering the ethical quality of acts.

Richardson's *Pamela* (1740) first revealed the possibilities, as a reflection of actual life and character, of the new fiction developed by Defoe. Superficially it resembled the romance of roguery in the choice of a heroine in service and in attention to commonplace detail. In all else the contrast to the picaresque novel was notable, and Richardson's other novels only emphasized it.

Fielding was by temperament and experience better fitted to profit from the picaresque tradition. His sensibilities were not too fine; his sense of humor was highly developed, and every-day life with its misadventures, slips from virtue, and comfortable animalism appealed to him. Richardson seemed to Fielding a milksop; so, after having tried his hand at twenty-five rather boisterous comedies, he undertook a fresh form and burlesqued *Pamela* in *Joseph Andrews*. *Joseph Andrews* is not as a whole a picaresque novel, because roguery does not predominate in the story. For all its practical jests and Spanish inspiration it is not completely picaresque, because the hero and heroine are impeccable, and the slips from virtue of Lady Booby and Mrs. Slipslop are only hinted at. Only in the career of Joseph's father is there an approach to a career of rascality. The chief reminiscences of the picaresque type in it are the menial station of Joseph, Mrs. Slipslop, and Fanny, and the peripatetic character of the adventures.

In *Tom Jones* the influence of the picaresque novel was diffused and transformed. If Jones contrasts with the hero of romance by being human, he contrasts with the picaresque anti-hero by being humane. He is warm-hearted and generous, but also weak-willed and something of a scapegrace, a compromise between the picaro and the hero, intended by his creator to set forth average humanity. The satire in *Tom Jones* is expended on individual types rather than on professions as in the picaresque novel, and the service of masters as an instrument of satire is discarded. The comic spirit here rises from farce to the highest comedy of character; realism subserves the ends of art, and the field of observation is wider than that of any picaresque novel. Romantic love, too, plays a conspicuous part; morality is made a matter of motive rather than of external prescription; and in place of giving a frightful example to warn the reader into avoiding evil courses, Fielding teaches sympathy with virtue, contempt for meanness, and indulgence for frailties. *Tom Jones*, though it could scarcely have come into being without picaresque predecessors, transcends them all, and cannot itself be ranked with the literature of roguery, notwithstanding such characters as Blifil, Thwackum and Square, Lady Bellaston, and Ensign Northerton. The inspiration of *Don Quixote* remained potent, especially in the quality of the humor and the person of Partridge; but it was now an influence diffused.

We have seen that the picaresque novel and the burlesque romance tended to combine in the hands of such writers as Scarron, Furetière, and Lesage, and that there are elements of both forms in Cervantes and Fielding. Satire was not originally a necessary characteristic of picaresque novels, and many of them were completely devoid of it. The English romance of roguery prior to Fielding had been peculiarly lacking in satire. It was through Fielding, indeed, that satire entered the English romance of roguery. Although *Joseph Andrews* is not wholly picaresque, it contains a strong infusion of picaresque elements, combined with satire of human frailties and vices. It is true that Fielding drew away more and more in *Tom Jones* and *Amelia* from sheer satire and the picaresque; yet he introduced the satirical romance of roguery into English literature.

The character sketch, the most prolific form in English and French literature of the seventeenth century, has a direct bearing on the development of the novel. It described a person who embodied a virtue, a vice, or some idiosyncrasy obnoxious to ridicule. One character was frequently contrasted with another, as in the novel, and as a frame to the portrait, biography and adventure were added. Addison and Steele, in *The Spectator*, created the character of Sir Roger de Coverley and almost transformed the character sketch into the novel of London and provincial life. From *The Spectator*, the character sketch, with its types and minute observation and urbane ridicule, passed into the novel and became a part of it. The character sketch, then, came from Addison and Steele to Fielding fully developed. He adopted the essayists' point of view of general, in distinction from personal satire. In the essayists Fielding found ready constructed for him the scenes most suitable for his novels: the playhouse, the masquerade, and the squire's country seat.

The character sketch of the seventeenth century differed from all that had preceded it in that whereas formerly the character sketch had been embodied in some other form, it was during that centurv wholly isolated from all that could hinder its independent development.[1] This accounts for the importance of the character sketch as a factor in the evolution of the novel. The character writers turned from the dignified impersonalities of the chivalric romances, and from the conscienceless scapegraces of the *roman bourgeois*, to a more minute analysis of character in what may be called its static condition. They regarded it, not as influenced by the interaction of other characters, but in and for itself. The result was a short account of the properties, qualities, or peculiarities which serve to individualize a type.

In spite of its limitations, the character sketch was, with the progress of the seventeenth century, slowly gaining greater freedom of form and thereby approaching more nearly to the fullness of development which it reached in the hands of Addison. For it was in the periodical essay that the character persisted longest as a distinct literary form. This is not strange when we consider how close the relation between the essay and the character had always been—owing, in part, to the difficulty the essayists of the seven-

[1] Edward C. Baldwin, *The Character Books of the 17th Century, in Relation to the Development of the Novel*, in *The Western Reserve University Bulletin*, October, 1900.

teenth century had in creating definite character without having recourse to the character sketch.

The periodical essay reached its highest development in *The Spectator*. In the second issue of *The Spectator* appeared six character sketches of those mythical gentlemen supposed to be associated with the Spectator as editors. These are six types of contemporary society: the country squire, the wealthy merchant, the young man of fashion, the soldier, the clergyman, and the bachelor of the Inner Temple. In these characters the change which has come over the old formal character sketch is apparent. From the old character sketch, every eccentricity of individual manner, every whimsical personal trait, all that which surprises and by its very inconsistency gives life to a literary portrait, had been rigidly excluded, as likely to rob it of its generic quality. But here the portrait is individualized, while still enabling us to recognize the type. These sketches, written by men who were more interested in the individual than the type, gave the formal character sketch its death blow.

Sir Roger de Coverley, as portrayed in the twenty-six papers recording his adventures, opinions, and conversations, is the character in whom the character sketch most closely approaches the novel. Even after the appearance of the *Coverley Papers*, when, as Taine says, the novel had unconsciously been discovered, there was no realization that a new form of art had been created. The faithful descriptions of life and manners and the feeling for character and incident were there; the essays needed but to have been thrown into the form of a continuous narrative to have given us the modern novel. Macaulay said that he had not the least doubt "that if Addison had written a novel on an extensive plan, it would have been superior to any that we possess." As it was, *The Spectator* prepared the way for the novel, for, with its circulation of thirty thousand copies, it had an incalculable influence in forming public taste in that direction.

Just how much the novel owes directly to the character sketch through *The Spectator* is impossible to determine. Fielding was familiar with the work of the periodical essayists, with whom his critical satire so closely allied him; Sir Roger de Coverley is midway between Overbury's country gentleman and Squire Western of *Tom Jones*. All three are individualized types, though they differ in the degree of individualization. Surely we may assume that Fielding was indebted to Addison for suggestions for character portrayal. The essential difference between the methods of the character writers and those of Richardson and Fielding is not that the former were concerned with types and the latter with individuals, for both aimed to portray types,[1] but that the former described characters which were fixed, statuesque, while the latter developed characters progressively. Like the character writers, they took an ordinary typical character, placed it in an ordinary situation, and then, imaginatively, yet realistically and precisely, exhibited each step of its mental and moral development. This was the new element which the novelists of the eighteenth century introduced into the portrayal of character. With its introduction the old formal character sketch disappeared as a separate literary form.

For methods of planning, developing, and unfolding his plots and presenting his characters, Fielding turned to the drama. He is particularly indebted to the comedy of manners, the light, gay, and burlesque comedy of Molière and Congreve. The elements borrowed from the drama he welded into his new kind of writing. The differences between the novel and the drama are not fundamental, and Fielding's genius was adapted to both forms. His early career as a dramatist gave him practice in the direct presentation of character and the management of plot, and these he employed in his novels, making them at once novels of character and dramatic novels. He delighted, as is shown by his digressions, in the freedom from the conventions of comedy afforded by the novel. He was conscious that his novels were dramatic, his characters being projected on the stage of his imagination, instead of an actual one, and often speaks of them as imaginative dramas. Better than any previous English fiction, they show that

[1] Fielding, in *Joseph Andrews*, Book III, Chapter I, tells us that he describes in his characters "not men but manners, not an individual but a species."

the novel as well as the drama can deal with the great human passions.

Fielding was familiar with Molière's comedies through his adaptation of *L'Avare*, which remarkably preserves the comic and satirical spirit of the original. His own plays and novels display a similar comedy and satire. No evidence of direct borrowing from Molière appears in Fielding's original writings, but no doubt Molière contributed something to Fielding's theory of comedy, particularly to his theory of affectation as the source of the ridiculous.[1]

The English comedy of manners contributed more heavily to Fielding's theory of the novel. From it, as well as from the periodical essay, he took his practice of presenting typical characters, the town fop, the country squire, the hypocritical and immoral great lady. His boisterous farcical scenes and the construction of his plots, their arrangement in separate, dramatic, comic scenes, are distinctly reminiscent of Restoration comedy, which he had imitated in his plays. A short discussion of Restoration comedy will most satisfactorily clarify this relationship.

Etherege is the first important writer of Restoration comedy. His comedies are the product of an age for which life was a pageant, incuriously observed, uncritically accepted, stuff for a finished epigram. Etherege found a form for the spirit of his age, wherein lies his greatest value. He has little relation to either Molière or Jonson. Nowhere in his plays is there evident the corrective laugh of the intellectual satirist or the grave purpose and intentness of mind which we find in comedies like Molière's. Etherege's comedies are most notable for their style, the light, witty, man-about-town flavor which so faithfully reflected the tone of "high life" in the late seventeenth century. This the other comic dramatists copied from him, and this Fielding received indirectly from him. He was the originator of the urbane wit, the realistic, gentlemanly speech, which characterizes Restoration

[1] Ethel M. Thornbury interestingly develops this point in her recent publication, *Fielding's Theory of the Comic Prose Epic*, in the *University of Wisconsin Studies in Language and Literature*, No. 30, 1931.

comedy, and which Fielding imitated in the dialogue of his plays and novels.

Wycherley is the satirist of the English comedy of manners. He alone of the comic dramatists shares in the spirit of Molière. He is witty, severely satirical, and brisk and powerful in his dialogue. Occasionally his satire lapses into downright moral fury, his hatred of the vices of his time violently breaking out. He seems fundamentally a Puritan, not born a gentleman of the Restoration, but made one by force of circumstance. The cynicism of *The Country Wife* and *The Plain Dealer* is not the expression of one reveling in vice, but of one who hates and satirizes it. These plays are, in point of view, purely comic, not lewd as Macaulay thought. Restoration comedy rested upon the comic treatment of sex, depending for its effect upon the elimination of passion. Its appeal is to the intelligence, not to the senses.

In his manly exuberance and savage satire, Wycherley, more than any other Restoration dramatist, reminds us of Fielding. Fielding has his wit, his power, his satirical and boisterously farcical spirit. Wycherley reminds us of Fielding's statement that he will hold up vice to ridicule. Fielding's theory of satire probably owes something to the plays of Wycherley. In *The Country Wife* are several types of characters which Fielding later used in his plays and novels. Wycherley's middle-aged, hypocritical, amorous women, Lady Fidget, Mrs. Dainty Fidget, and Mrs. Squeamish, resemble Lady Booby and Lady Bellaston. His town beaus and fops, Mr. Horner, Mr. Harcourt, Mr. Dorilant, and Mr. Sparkish, remind us of Lord Fellamar and Beau Didapper. Fielding owes something to Wycherley for these characters, which the latter had helped to make typical of Restoration comedy. The broadly farcical scenes of *The Country Wife*, also, recall the boisterous scenes in *Joseph Andrews* and *Tom Jones*.

Congreve, the greatest of the comic dramatists of the Restoration, was influenced by Etherege in his style and by Wycherley in the severity and vividness of his portraiture. He was their natural and perfect heir, raising both their arts to a higher plane and imparting polish and artistic finish to the comedy of manners.

Though more limited in their scope, his plays are as perfect pictures of his time as the novels of Fielding are of his. He carries Etherege's urbane, gentlemanly manner and Wycherley's wit and point to their highest possible expression. His style has always been highly praised. Hazlitt says of it, "The style of Congreve is inimitable, nay perfect. It is the highest model of comic dialogue. Every sentence is replete with sense and satire, conveyed in the most polished and pointed terms." Meredith says, "Where Congreve excels all his English rivals is in his literary force and a succinctness of style peculiar to him. He hits the mean of a fine style and a natural in dialogue. He is at once precise and voluble." Congreve's style set the standard which Fielding tried to reach in his comic dialogue.

Congreve's masterpiece, *The Way of the World*, is a perfect expression of the temperament by which life is accepted and observed, not as a problem, but as a pageant. In it, Congreve exhibits a calm and finished superiority to all life can offer of good or bad. It is the final assertion of that high-minded indifference which began with Etherege, in accepting and enjoying the vicissitudes of fortune, and ended, with Congreve, in despising them. The formula of the comedy of manners is raised to its most perfect embodiment in this play.

Fielding accepted this formula in his plays, and it later influenced his conception of the novel. We find evidence of this in *The Way of the World*, in typical characters and situations, which are the prototypes of characters and situations found in Fielding. Sir Wilful Witwoud is an early study of the country squire, whose ignorance, crude rusticity, and warm heart are preserved in Squire Badger of Fielding's *Don Quixote in England* and Squire Western of *Tom Jones*. Lady Wishfort, the amorous old hypocrite of *The Way of the World*, has her counterparts in Lady Booby of *Joseph Andrews* and Lady Bellaston of *Tom Jones*. Foible, the maid to Lady Wishfort, resembles, in her garrulous vulgarity, both Mrs. Slipslop, Lady Booby's maid, and Mrs. Honour, Sophia Western's maid. Two parallel situations in *The Way of the World* and *Tom Jones* are those in which Mirabell pretends love for Lady Wishfort and Tom Jones for Lady Bellaston.

The Way of the World expresses best that antithesis found in the plays of Etherege and Wycherley between the true wit and the false. In ridiculing the false wit Congreve's theory of satire is like Fielding's. In his dedication of *The Way of the World*, he says, "Those characters which are meant to be ridiculed in most of our comedies, are fools so gross, that, in my humble opinion, they should rather disturb than divert the well-natured and reflecting part of an audience; they are rather objects of charity than contempt; and instead of moving our mirth, they ought very often to excite our compassion. This reflexion moved me to design some characters which should appear ridiculous, not so much through a natural folly (which is incorrigible, and therefore improper for the stage) as through an affected wit; a wit which at the same time that it is affected, is also false." Congreve ridicules affectation in false wits; Fielding makes it the source of the "true ridiculous" in the Author's Preface to *Joseph Andrews*. He probably owes something to Congreve for this theory of satire. Another passage recalling Fielding's discussion of the ridiculous appears in Congreve's *Essay on Humour*, in his letter to John Dennis written in 1695. "For my part I am as willing to laugh as anybody, and as easily diverted with an object truly ridiculous; but at the same time I never care for seeing things that force me to entertain low thoughts of my nature. . . I could never look long upon a monkey without very mortifying reflections. . . I think the follies (with which we are diverted) should be only such as men's humour may incline them to, and not follies entirely abstracted from both humour and nature." Similarly, Fielding, in the Author's Preface to *Joseph Andrews*, says that deformity, misfortune, or calamity should not be ridiculed. Congreve, then, furnished a model of satire for Fielding, as well as a model of style.

The comic point of view of Etherege, Wycherley, and Congreve was condemned in the moral reaction which followed the publication in 1697 of Collier's *A Short View of the Profaneness and*

Immorality of the English Stage. Collier revived the moral test for plays. Before the *Short View* the public was apparently blind to the sinfulness of its theatre. Afterward, the point of view of critics and public was completely changed, and we find Addison and Steele using the moral test upon the drama. Steele's criterion was this: "A good play acted before a well-bred audience must raise very proper incitements to good behaviour and be the most quick and most prevailing method of giving young people a turn of sense and breeding."[1]

The loss of the comic point of view meant the gradual death of the comedy of manners. Although Vanbrugh, Farquhar, and Fielding followed the formula of Congreve, except for occasional bursts, they lost the purely comic spirit. Fielding, though essentially a comic genius, adopted with his age the purpose of moral instruction as well as of entertainment. The moral reaction to Restoration drama helped to make Fielding a moralist as well as a comic writer. If he had lived in the time of Wycherley, he might have given his comic genius fuller rein. In the eighteenth century, "true comedy melted away into the sweetness of tears, or shattered itself upon the pointless crudities of Fielding. . . Collier and the censorship had between them effectively done their work."[2] It was no longer possible to treat the old subjects of the comedy of manners in a comic way. The ban upon the comic treatment of sex and marriage made Fielding choose inferior subjects in his plays, which were often "pointless crudities." In them he was working not only an exhausted vein, but a vein which the new critical point of view made it impossible to work profitably.

Vanbrugh belonged to the new period which followed Collier's *Short View* and ushered in the eighteenth century. But he accepted Restoration comedy for his model, at the same time adopting a moral definition of the function of comedy. "The business of comedy is to show people what they should do by representing them upon the stage doing what they should not.

[1] *The Tatler* for 26 November, 1709.

[2] B. Dobrée, *Restoration Drama*, p.169.

The stage is a glass for the world to view itself in. People ought therefore to see themselves as they are; if it makes their faces too fair, they won't know they are dirty, and by consequence will neglect to wash 'em." In *The Provoked Wife* we find racy humor predominating in an atmosphere which is anything but morally instructive. He is not as careful to teach virtue and condemn vice as his definition would indicate, and this play is therefore out of harmony with his age. His humor, which is his most attractive feature, is at times quite like Fielding's in its turn for the broadly farcical in character and situation. The episode in *The Provoked Wife* where Sir John Brute is disguised as his wife recalls the rough farce in *Joseph Andrews*, such as the nocturnal adventures in Booby Hall. The masked rendezvous in Spring Gardens, when Constant and Heartfree meet Lady Brute and her niece Belinda, recalls the masquerade in *Tom Jones*, when Tom meets Lady Bellaston. The town fops and rakes, such as Lord Rake and Sir John Brute, resemble characters like Lord Fellamar in Fielding. Next to Wycherley, among these comic dramatists, the comic spirit of Fielding seems most closely allied to that of Vanbrugh. Fielding was familiar with Vanbrugh's comedies, referring favorably to them in his novels. His theory of the function of comedy is probably influenced by Vanbrugh, whose discussion of this point recalls Fielding's, both justifying their portrayal of bad characters and vice by saying that they will thus teach men to be good.

The comedy of manners, reaching perfection in Congreve, perceptibly droops in Vanbrugh, and is extinguished in Farquhar, who contributed its last brilliant examples. Like Vanbrugh, he accepted an outgrown convention. His temperament and environment were like those of his moral nineteenth century critics, yet he tried to write comedies like Congreve's. His consequent inconsistencies, often resulting in serious moral and artistic offences, are more patent than Vanbrugh's, for Farquhar was a more careless writer. He was a middle-class professional author, and in accepting the gentlemanly tradition of Etherege, he expressed himself in a foreign language.

Farquhar's *Discourse upon Comedy* shows the decay of the comic idea. He gives a definition of comedy of which Collier himself might approve: "a well-framed tale handsomely told as an agreeable vehicle for counsel or reproof." He says that Aesop was the first comedian. "Where should we seek for a foundation but in Aesop's symbolical way of moralising upon tales and fables, with this difference, that his stories were shorter than ours?" Whatever difference time had made in the form, we must stick to the end and intention of Aesop's *Fables*, which was to school mankind into better manners. The inconsistencies to which this moral purpose would give rise when applied to Restoration comedy are obvious. We are reminded again of Fielding's statements of his moral purpose, which led him into similar inconsistencies in *Joseph Andrews* and *Tom Jones*.[1]

While Fielding accepted the formula of the comedy of manners for his plays, he created characters which are not merely wooden imitations of the types in Restoration comedy. Even when the outlines of the type are preserved, the reality of his characters gives one a foretaste of his mature powers. In his first play, *Love in Several Masques*, we have two such characters, Sir Positive Trap and Lord Formal. A tribute to the originality of his characters is that his critics more often seek their originals among real people than in literature. Squire Badger, in *Don Quixote in England*, one of the most successful of Fielding's early portraits, is the first sketch of Squire Western of *Tom Jones*. In this play, Guzzle, the innkeeper, Brief, the lawyer, and Drench, the physician, also foreshadow characters in the novels.

The Coffee House Politician has comic force and little sentimentality. Its humor has some of the flavor of the novels. The dishonest justice and the coffee-house politician "are elaborated with a richness of detail and a vigour of satire scarcely found on the stage since Shadwell's imitations of Ben Jonson."[2] *The Modern Husband*, Fielding's most ambitious drama, was a sincere but

[1] For example, Parson Adams's adventures with Parson Trulliber, and Tom Jones's discovery of Square in Molly Seagrim's garret, while highly comic, and good satire, are too coarse to be in the narrow sense morally edifying.

[2] A. H. Thorndike, *English Comedy*, p.372.

futile effort to revive satirical comedy. Its presentation of manners delighted Lady Mary Montagu, but displeased the Drury Lane audiences. *The Universal Gallant* was vigorously and perhaps justly damned. Its chief scene suggests Fielding's fondness for farcical extravagance, a quality he inherited in part from Wycherley and Vanbrugh, and shows his failure to distinguish between comic scenes suitable to the stage and those suitable to the novel.

The Wedding Day, Fielding's last comedy, is witty, but carelessly built on the formula, which he vigorously condemns in *Tom Jones*, of lewdness for four acts and virtue in the last, and contains sentiment and humor badly mixed. By this time *Joseph Andrews* was successfully ridiculing *Pamela*, and one feels that, as Macklin said to Fielding in his prologue to this play,

> "You'd better stuck to Abraham Adams by half;
> He, in spite of critics, can make your readers laugh."

Arthur Murphy said of this play that if Fielding "had resolved to shape the business and characters of his last comedy into the form of a novel, there is not one scene in the piece which, in his hands, would not have been very susceptible of ornament; but as they are arranged at present in dramatic order, there are few of them from which the taste and good sense of an audience ought not, with propriety, to revolt."

Fielding failed as a dramatist in that he never learned to please his audiences. "It was not in his temperament, as it was in [Colley] Cibber's, to adjust lewdness and sentiment in such proportions as to excite and edify a capricious public; and it was not within his skill to confine his humour to what could be represented effectively by an actor."[1] His wit and humor were never trained to the regular measures of high comedy. Part of his failure must be attributed to a theatre that demanded farce and burlesque, but gave no encouragement to comedy after the fashion of the old masters; yet one wonders that so great a humorist could write such paltry comedies. His comedies fail in both humor and morality. They added no fresh humor, and their immorality offended an audi-

[1] A. H. Thorndike, *English Comedy*, p.375.

ence that had been pleased by sentiment. As a revolt against sentimentality they were impotent. The exhaustion of the vein of Restoration comedy appears in the failure of so brilliant a wit as Fielding to produce anything comparable to the plays of Congreve and Vanbrugh.

As popular literature, the drama was superseded in the eighteenth century by the pamphlet, the periodical, and the novel. Sentimentalism throve, not in the plays of Steele and Cibber, but in the novels of Richardson. Prose fiction and not the drama provided the opportunity for Fielding's genius. Since the Elizabethans, English comedy has not shown a great wealth of characterization. The novel has proved superior in exhibiting the humors of mankind. Literature has not had a successor to Ben Jonson in the drama, but it has had Smollett and Fielding, Scott and Dickens. The novel, moreover, has presented the average persons of life in a fashion impossible on the stage. In this the novels of Fielding surpass the comedy of manners, though indebted to it for their dialogue, typical characters, and dramatic structure. Their wealth of characterization, their portrayal of the average persons of life, is beyond anything in Restoration comedy. Yet Fielding's method of character presentation is essentially that of the dramatist, learned from his own practice in imitating Restoration drama. "Fielding puts his characters before us by making them speak and act; he makes them expose their essential traits in the first few syllables uttered. The character drawing is in the dialogue itself, and the dialogue is always shapely literature."[1]

Fielding's familiarity with the Greek and Latin poets, historians, and critics played a considerable part in forming his conception of the novel. His repeated reference in the novels to classical authors is evidence of this. Like most men of his age, he was an admirer of Homer, and his theory of the "comic epic poem in prose," stated in the preface to *Joseph Andrews*, is founded, he says, upon Aristotle's criticism of Homer in *The Poetics*.[2] He

[1] E. A. Baker, *The History of the English Novel*, vol. IV, p.97.

[2] An excellent account of Fielding's debt to the epic tradition, ancient and modern, is found in Ethel M. Thornbury's *Fielding's Theory of the Comic Prose Epic*, *University of Wisconsin Studies in Language and Literature*, No. 30, 1931.

frequently cites Homer and Aristotle in *Joseph Andrews* in support of his critical theories, and burlesques Homer in his mock-heroic battles. Lucian, another favorite author, is mentioned as a model for Fielding's burlesques and parodies. Plutarch, Nepos, Virgil, and Juvenal appear as authorities and models for his methods as historian and satirist. In *Tom Jones*, allusions to Homer and Aristotle to support his practices are again frequent. Free quotation from the ancients is justified, he thinks, by their wealth and fame, though we must respect the rights of moderns in their works. Horace's rules are often invoked to reinforce Fielding's critical opinions, and with Aristotle and Longinus, Horace is recognized as an authoritative critic. Socrates, Cicero, Cato, Ovid, Seneca, Aeschines, Lucian, Aristophanes, Demosthenes, Plutarch, and Terence are casually mentioned in *Tom Jones* as precedents for various devices and standards of authorship.

In his *Journal of a Voyage to Lisbon* Fielding makes a final significant confession about his interest in the classics. "I must confess," he says, "I should have honored and loved Homer more had he written a true history of his own times in humble prose than those noble poems which have so justly collected the praise of all ages; for, though I read these with more admiration and astonishment, I still read Herodotus, Thucydides, and Xenophon with more amusement and more satisfaction." Thus, at least at this time, "true history" in prose appealed more to him than the finest epic poetry. His style was professedly modeled after Lucian, and of the ancients he enjoyed the great prose writers most. This perhaps explains Fielding's desire to write a "comic epic" to take the place of the lost *Margites*, which he imagines to have been a "true history" in prose, as were his own novels.

Fielding nevertheless profited by his knowledge of the Homeric epic and formed his theory of the novel partly upon it. The greatest benefit which he gained through his reading of the epic and its critics was in the matter of form. As W. L. Cross says, "The great novelists since Fielding have taught the public that a novel must have a beginning and an end."[1] Fielding kept firmly in mind the Aristotelian principle of unity of action as applied to the epic, of which he considered his novels the modern counterpart. He knew the teaching of *The Poetics* that "the story ought obviously to be constructed dramatically, and be about a single action complete in itself, with a beginning, middle, and end, so that it may produce its own proper pleasure as if it were one complete living creature." This teaching Fielding endeavored to exemplify in his novels, a thing which no one had yet done, and in *Tom Jones* he came nearer to unity of action than had any previous novelist.

Fielding's easy familiarity with the classics made it natural for him to refer to them, both in discussing the principles of his art and in describing his characters and their actions. "What with some men is ostentation was in his case the simple application of materials which early habit had made so familiar that they had lost their learned air and were entirely native to him."[2] His wide reading is further attested by the books he left at his death.[3] To quote Austin Dobson, "He died possessed of an exceedingly well-chosen and 'polite' library of books, as varied in character as Johnson's, more extensive by far than Goldsmith's, and in the matter of those authors whom Moses Primrose describes comprehensively as 'the Ancients,' as richly endowed as that of Gray."[4] One notable feature of this library is the absence of fiction. It lacks even copies of *Le Paysan Parvenu* or the *Histoire de Marianne* of Marivaux, an author with whom he was fully acquainted, and by whom, as we have seen, he was in a measure influenced. If Fielding had few novels and romances, however, he was fairly furnished with poets; and, as became the author of *Pasquin* and *Tom Thumb*, he was rich in playwrights. In biography,

[1] W. L. Cross, *The Development of the English Novel*, p.25.

[2] Whitwell Elwin in *The Quarterly Review*, vol. xcviii, no. cxcv (Dec., 1855), p.102, reprinted in his *Some XVIII Century Men of Letters*, vol. ii, p.86.

[3] A verbatim copy of the pamphlet in the British Museum containing a list of Fielding's library is included in Ethel M. Thornbury's *Fielding and the Comic Prose Epic*.

[4] Austin Dobson, Fielding's Library in *Eighteenth Century Vignettes*, p.167.

science, philosophy, and theology, he had many standard works. But his largest and most important sections were in law and classical literature. His collection of Greek and Latin classics had considerable variety and range. "When it is found that in his youth Fielding had been a fervent student of the classics, that he remained throughout life a voracious reader; and that his works everywhere afford confirmation of both these things, it is perhaps not unreasonable to conclude that he made good use of the large collection of Greek and Latin authors which he left behind him at his death, and that he was, in reality, the scholar he has been affirmed to be."[1]

In acknowledging Fielding's debt to the classics, however, it would be well not to take it more seriously than he did himself. For all his classical reading and serious reliance on critical principles derived from Homer, Aristotle, Horace, and others, Fielding often made fun of "the ancients" and of those who took them too seriously. His burlesques of Homer and his flippant references to Aristotle show that his attitude toward them is a mingling of respect and good-natured amusement. The much debated controversy between ancients and moderns, celebrated in *The Battle of the Books*, had aroused his scorn and amusement at those who were over-zealous in the cause of the ancients. Preserving a balanced attitude, he could profit by the virtues of the classics and at the same time laugh heartily at them.

[1] Austin Dobson, Fielding's Library, in *Eighteenth Century Vignettes*, p.177.

II

THE THEORY OF JOSEPH ANDREWS

THE old romances had failed in their art, their plots being loose and episodic. The picaresque stories had a beginning, but no end; they too became episodic and ended sometimes only with the death of the author. The romancers and picaresque story-tellers had no clearly defined conception of what a novel should be, as an independent and organic literary species. From them to Defoe, Richardson, and Fielding the transition is from a struggling and misdirected literary form to a well-defined species. But these early writers contributed something to the development of the novel, for, as W. L. Cross says, "From the Arthurian Romance and the Fabliau downward, in the eternal swing between idealism and realism, there is a continuous growth, an accumulation of incidents, situations, characters, and experiments in structure, much of which was a legacy to the Eighteenth Century."[1] Out of these earlier sources the novel of character and the novel of incident of the eighteenth century finally evolved, because of the growing demand that the novel should have orderly structure and be a careful study, either of some phase of real life, or of conduct in a situation which the imagination is willing to accept for the time being.

Robinson Crusoe (1719) is the earliest English novel of incident. It differed from the picaresque story in being an elaboration of contemporary incident fascinating to the imagination. The author invested his narrative with a sense of reality by using actual memoirs with the accompaniment of a fictitious diary. Defoe humanized adventure. His novel carried the middle-class message: be patient, honest, and industrious, and you will be rewarded. Defoe's greatest distinction is in attaining verisimilitude

[1] W. L. Cross, *The Development of the English Novel*, p.27.

through minute detail and the unadorned language of everyday life. Bunyan was his forerunner in realism, and his successor was Swift. These three writers usher in a new era for the novel and are the sources to which even romance returns for instruction from Scott to Stevenson.

Richardson achieved the second great imaginative success in the novel in making his men and women and their environments more complete and real, discovering the art of the novel of character. Richardson's novel of character is psychological, a revealing of states of feeling in acts. Something of the allegory of the old romances survives in Richardson's characters, and he owes much to the drama for his characters and plots. *Pamela* is bourgeois comedy, *Clarissa*, bourgeois tragedy. Richardson gave Europe what it long had wanted, a form of literature that adequately presented life as it is, united with an ideal of life as it ought to be. He created four new literary types: the polished rake, the immaculate gentleman, the chaste woman, and the Protestant martyr. To him the world is indebted for the epistolary novel, and his influence on the content of the novel is great.

As we have seen, Fielding was familiar with the Greek and Latin poets, historians, and critics. He had absorbed the spirit of the great European humorists: Aristophanes, Lucian, Cervantes, Rabelais, Shakespeare, Molière, Swift, and Lesage. He had observed life closely, as his comedies show. In them he satirized the contemporary drama and politics, and in his first novel, *Joseph Andrews*, he set out to parody contemporary literature as exemplified by Richardson's *Pamela*. He played Cervantes to Richardson's Montemayor. As he wrote *Joseph Andrews*, the parody slipped from him, for he became deeply interested in his characters and his "new kind of writing."

In form *Joseph Andrews* is a series of adventures in high and low life, divided into books which have mock-heroic introductions, and diversified by episodes It has its prototype in the burlesque adventures by Cervantes and Scarron, and in the picaresque novel as refined by Lesage in *Gil Blas*. Fielding called it a "comic epic," having in mind the lost *Margites* of Homer, a dramatic epic in which comedy was secondary. Fielding reversed the process by investing comedy with epic proportions and, as more suitable to his age, writing in prose instead of verse.

Conscious of being the originator of a new kind of writing, Fielding felt called upon to define it explicitly. He states his theories concerning it in the Author's Preface and in the introductory chapters to the Books into which the novel is divided. At the beginning of the Author's Preface he addresses his readers: "As it is possible the mere English reader may have a different idea of romance from the author of these little volumes, and may consequently expect a kind of entertainment not to be found, nor which was even intended, in the following pages, it may not be improper to premise a few words concerning this kind of writing, which I do not remember to have seen hitherto attempted in our language."

He begins by relating his novel to the classical epic: "The Epic, as well as the Drama, is divided into tragedy and comedy. Homer, who was the father of this species of poetry, gave us a pattern of both these, though that of the latter kind is entirely lost; which Aristotle tells us, bore the same relation to comedy which his *Iliad* bears to tragedy." This loss, he adds, accounts for the lack of imitations of Homer's comic epic among the ancients. Extending still further the field of the epic, he says:

> As this poetry may be tragic or comic, I will not scruple to say it may be likewise either in verse or prose: for though it wants one particular, which the critic enumerates in the constituent parts of an epic poem, namely metre; yet when any kind of writing contains all its other parts, such as fable, action, characters, sentiments, and diction, and is deficient in metre only, it seems, I think, reasonable to refer it to the epic; at least, as no critic hath thought proper to range it under any other head, or to assign it a particular name for itself.

Fielding here takes advantage of his innovation by affixing to his work a name of dignified and splendid traditions. Except for metre, *Joseph Andrews* really contained all the elements of the epic, as defined by eighteenth century critics, which doubtless suggested to Fielding that he might in good faith, and profitably, appropriate the name. He effectively justifies its use when he says:

> It is much fairer and more reasonable to give it [the prose epic] a name common with that species from which it differs only in a single instance, than to confound it with those which it resembles in no other. Such are those voluminous works commonly called Romances, namely, *Clelia*, *Cleopatra*, *Astraea*, *Cassandra*, the *Grand Cyrus*, and innumerable others, which contain, as I apprehend, very little instruction or entertainment.

His scorn for the romances reveals that his own writing is, like the picaresque novel and burlesque romance, in reaction against their extravagances. His implication is that the epic, in prose or verse, presents real life, while the romance does not.

Next, in the Author's Preface, we come to a fuller definition of Fielding's kind of novel. "Now, a comic romance is a comic epic poem in prose; differing from comedy, as the serious epic from tragedy: its action being more extended and comprehensive, containing a much larger circle of incidents, and introducing a greater variety of characters." He understands the close relationship between the drama and the novel, their differences being quantitative mainly, differences of extent, of number, of variety. He recognizes the close analogy between the comedy in drama and his comic romance in fiction, both containing the same elements. Further distinctions follow:

> It differs from the serious romance in its fable and action, in this; that as in the one these are grave and solemn, so in the other they are light and ridiculous; it differs in its characters by introducing persons of inferior rank, and consequently of inferior manners, whereas, the grave romance sets the highest before us: lastly in its sentiments and diction; by preserving the ludicrous instead of the sublime. In the diction, I think, burlesque itself may be sometimes admitted; of which many instances will occur in this work, as in the description of the battles, and some other places, not necessary to be pointed out to the classical reader, for whose entertainment those parodies or burlesque imitations are chiefly calculated.

This comparison is no doubt ironic. His previous scornful reference to the serious romance would indicate that by its "grave and solemn" fable and action he implies its dullness and heaviness. Similarly, the statement that only "the highest" persons are set before us is a reflection of his amusement at the snobbishness of the romance tradition, and the reference to "the sublime" in the romances is ridicule of their stilted affectation in sentiments and diction.

The qualities here ascribed to the "comic romance" are found in the picaresque novel and the burlesque romance, either of which might be substituted for it in this comparison. Burlesque diction naturally appears in the burlesque romance, though not in the picaresque story, being used in *Don Quixote* for direct ridicule of the serious romance. In burlesquing Homer, Fielding reveals his classical learning by his familiarity with Homer's diction.

Fielding next distinguishes his "comic romance" from pure burlesque.

> But though we have sometimes admitted this [burlesque] in our diction, we have carefully excluded it from our sentiments and characters; for there it is never properly introduced, unless in writings of the burlesque kind, which this is not intended to be. Indeed, no two species of writing can differ more widely than the comic and the burlesque; for as the latter is ever the exhibition of what is monstrous and unnatural, and where our delight, if we examine it, arises from the surprizing absurdity, as in appropriating the manners of the highest to the lowest, or *è converso*; so in the former we should ever confine ourselves strictly to nature, from the just imitation of which will flow all the pleasure we can in this way convey to a sensible reader.

Here Fielding deviates in theory from the burlesque romances and reduces his debt to Cervantes, whose inspiration he had already acknowledged. We have already pointed out the similarities and differences between the art of Cervantes and that of Fielding. Though in *Joseph Andrews* Fielding imitated "the manner of Cervantes," he departs from it in more closely following nature, and in not burlesquing characters or sentiments. The commonplace rule of following nature is adopted by Fielding partly from the realistic examples of the picaresque novel, the epic tradition, which he absorbed from his classical reading, the comedy of manners, and the character essay. These influences and Fielding's naturally practical and observant genius combined to form the creed of realism which is the principal basis of his art. His talent for close observation of life made him the logical heir of the realistic tradition. Some of his critics tend to discount the literary sources of his realism. Banerji, a recent critic, says, "The practical temper of the age and his genius helped him to collect the right materials and make the best use of them. His debt to literary predecessors is small compared to his debt to experience."[1] We should be wrong, however, in assuming that Fielding's novels could have been written without these literary predecessors to pave the way for him. Fielding was so widely read and so familiar with the literary sources previously discussed that it seems erroneous to assume that his art is predominantly original.

To the statement of his realistic purpose Fielding adds that the comic writer should be least excused for deviating from nature, for, though the serious writer cannot always meet with the great and admirable, "life everywhere furnishes an accurate observer with the ridiculous." He presses the distinction between "mere burlesque" and the "comic romance" by clearing up the confusion attending the use of the term "burlesque," insisting that "a certain drollery in stile, where characters and sentiments are perfectly natural, no more constitutes the burlesque, than an empty pomp and dignity of words, where everything else is mean and low, can entitle any performance to the appellation of the true sublime." In other words, occasional burlesque diction does not make a work "burlesque," when the characters and sentiments are realistic.

Fielding's debt to the classics for his "comic romance" theory is indicated by a quotation from Lord Shaftsbury, in which, speaking of mere burlesque, Shaftsbury said, "There is no such thing to be found in the writings of the ancients." Fielding ex-

[1] H. K. Banerji, *The Life and Works of Fielding*, p.12.

cluded burlesque characters and sentiments partly by the example of "the ancients." He confesses some liking for pure burlesque, however, because "it contributes more to exquisite mirth and laughter than any other [kind of writing]."

There follows an illustration of Fielding's distinction between burlesque and comic romance, in which he compares the works of a "comic history painter" with "those performances which the Italians call Caricatura," drawing analogies between comic writing and comic painting, both of which are based on "the exactest copying of nature," and burlesque writing and the Caricatura, in which "we allow all licence," its aim being "to exhibit monsters, not men," all "distortions and exaggerations whatever" being "within its proper province." Hogarth, whom Fielding greatly admired, is cited as the best "comic history painter." This distinction is of course obvious, but such clarification was necessary when, as Fielding said, there was such confusion in the use of these terms.

He then declares his satirical purpose. "The Ridiculous only . . . falls within my province in the present work," he says, proceeding to explain the term and how often it has been mistaken. One cannot properly ridicule "the blackest villanies," or "the most dreadful calamities." Aristotle tells us that the ridiculous is "proper to comedy," and that "villany is not its object"; but he does not say what it or its object is. "Nor doth the Abbé Bellegarde who hath written a treatise on this subject, though he shows us many species of it, once trace it to its fountain." Accordingly, Fielding states his definition.

The only source of the true Ridiculous (as it appears to me) is affectation. But though it arises from one spring only, when we consider the infinite streams into which this one branches, we shall presently cease to admire at the copious field it affords to an observer. Now, affectation proceeds from one of these two causes, vanity or hypocrisy: for as vanity puts us on affecting false characters, in order to purchase applause; so hypocrisy sets us on an endeavour to avoid censure, by concealing our vices under an appearance of their opposite virtues. And though these two causes are often confounded (for there is some difficulty in distin-

> guishing them), yet, as they proceed from very different motives, so they are as clearly distinct in their operations: for indeed, the affectation which arises from vanity is nearer to truth than the other, as it hath not that violent repugnancy of nature to struggle with, which that of the hypocrite hath. It may be likewise noted, that affectation doth not imply an absolute negation of those qualities which are affected; and, therefore, though, when it proceeds from hypocrisy, it be nearly allied to deceit; yet when it comes from vanity only, it partakes of the nature of ostentation: for instance, the affectation of liberality in a vain man differs visibly from the same affectation in the avaricious; for though the vain man is not what he would appear, or hath not the virtue he affects, to the degree he would be thought to have it; yet it sits less awkwardly on him than on the avaricious man, who is the very reverse of what he would seem to be.

This discussion is highly important, as it describes the theoretical basis for Fielding's satire. The satirical mood prevails in the novels, except *Amelia*, and from this point of view Fielding presents reality. He sees life clearly, but with a view to satirizing human frailties, particularly the affectations arising from vanity and hypocrisy. His satire is not unkind or merciless except to the blackest hypocrisy, and his laughter is usually sympathetic. In theory, it was doubtless evolved from Fielding's reading of the great satirists, Aristophanes, Lucian, Rabelais, Cervantes, Shakespeare, Jonson, Molière, and Swift, and from his own contempt for affectation, which he wished to laugh out of the world. Fielding's greatest imitator, Thackeray, might with perfect propriety have prefixed this theory of satire to his *Vanity Fair*, in which he has applied it throughout.

In the next paragraph of his Author's Preface Fielding proceeds with his definition of the ridiculous. "From the discovery of this affectation arises the Ridiculous, which always strikes the reader with surprize and pleasure; and that in a higher and stronger degree when the affectation arises from hypocrisy, than when from vanity; for to discover any one to be the exact reverse of what he affects, is more surprizing, and consequently more ridiculous, than to find him a little deficient in the quality he desires the reputation of." He adds that Ben Jonson, who understood the ridiculous best of all men, "hath chiefly used the hypocritical affectation." The pleasure arising from satire has never been more clearly described. The point that only affectation should be the source of ridicule is emphasized.

> Now from affectation only, the misfortunes and calamities of life, or the imperfections of nature, may become the objects of ridicule. Surely he hath a very ill-framed mind who can look on ugliness, infirmity, or poverty, as ridiculous in themselves: nor do I believe any man living who meets a dirty fellow riding through the streets in a cart, is struck with an idea of the ridiculous from it; but if he should see the same figure descend from a coach and six, or bolt from his chair with his hat under his arm, he would then begin to laugh, and with justice.

Fielding here recognizes that incongruity is an important element in the ridiculous. His definition might be criticized for not including all sorts of incongruity in the ridiculous, instead of only that arising from affectation; but he implies a distinction between the "true Ridiculous," which is to be literally ridiculed or satirized, and the merely humorous, arising from accidental incongruities in which there is no affectation.

The introduction of vices, apparently as the subject of ridicule, against his own rule, is explained as follows:

> First . . . it is very difficult to pursue a series of human actions and keep clear from them. Secondly . . . the vices to be found here are rather the accidental consequences of some human frailty or foible, than causes habitually existing in the mind. Thirdly . . . they are never set forth as objects of ridicule, but of detestation. Fourthly . . . they [vicious persons] are never the principal figure at that time on the scene: and lastly, they never produce the intended evil.

His first reason is sufficient, if we consider the sort of plot and characters Fielding chose and his resolute realism. His third reason might seem a contradiction of his statement that "the Ridiculous only . . . falls within my province in the present work." But in creating objects of ridicule, other objects must of course be introduced as a background, so that this earlier statement must not be taken too literally.

The next paragraph summarizes the argument of the Author's Preface and includes a few remarks on the characters. He again shows his consciousness of innovation by speaking of "this species of writing, which I have affirmed to be hitherto unattempted in our language." He disclaims any intention "to vilify or asperse any one" in the characters of the novel; "for though everything is copied from the book of nature, and scarce a character or action produced which I have not taken from my own observations and experience; yet I have used the utmost care to obscure the persons by such different circumstances, degrees, and colours, that it will be impossible to guess at them with any degree of certainty; and if it ever happens otherwise, it is only where the failure characterized is so minute, that it is a foible only which the party himself may laugh at as well as any other." Fielding had earlier got himself into trouble by aspersions in his plays upon political figures of his day. *The Historical Register* and *Pasquin*, aimed at Sir Robert Walpole, the Prime Minister, caused the closing of the theatres by the licensing act of 1737. Fielding was naturally anxious to avoid the failure of his novel through any libellous interpretation of its characters. Some of his critics have taken this passage as proof of the complete originality of his realism and the absence of any debt to literary predecessors. But everything might be "copied from the book of nature" and "taken from my own observations and experience," and still be formed upon realistic traditions and models.

The Author's Preface states the fundamental principles of Fielding's art, his general conception of the novel as a "comic epic poem in prose" and his theory of satire. Accordingly, the Preface has been extensively quoted, and these principles fully discussed.

We find further statements of Fielding's theory in the text of *Joseph Andrews*. In the first chapter, called Of Writing Lives in General, and Particularly of Pamela; with a Word by the bye of Colley Cibber and Others, we find a statement which, though it refers ironically to *Pamela* and, in this connection, to the *Apology for the Life of Colley Cibber*, expresses the positive side of Fielding's moral purpose in his novels. Like most eighteenth century authors he aimed to combine instruction with delight. One important means of instruction, the portrayal of noble and exemplary characters, he here describes.

> As it often happens that the best men are but little known, and consequently cannot extend the usefulness of their examples a great way, the writer may be called in aid to spread their history farther, and to present the amiable pictures to those who have not the happiness of knowing the originals; and so, by communicating such valuable patterns to the world, he may perhaps do a more extensive service to mankind than the person whose life originally afforded the pattern.

Chapter I of Book II, called Of Divisions in Authors, contains some observations on the division of novels into separate books and chapters. Fielding says that "In this as well as all other instances we consult the advantage of our reader, not our own." To designate the spaces between chapters he uses the figure of an inn, where the reader may stop and take refreshment and rest. The blank pages between his books, he says, "are to be regarded as those stages where in long journies the traveller stays some time to repose himself and consider of what he hath seen in the parts he hath already passed through." A volume without such places of rest "resembles the opening of wilds or seas, which tires the eye and fatigues the spirit when entered upon." The titles prefixed to every chapter are "but so many inscriptions over the gates of inns, . . . informing the readers what entertainment he is to expect, which if he likes not, he may travel on to the next. . ." These inscriptions are accurate indications of the contents of each chapter, unlike those of "the celebrated Montaigne, who promises you one thing and gives you another; nor some title-page authors, who promise a great deal and produce nothing at all." He adds a quaintly practical reason for his divisions: "It prevents spoiling the beauty of a book by turning down its leaves, a method otherwise necessary to those readers who (though they read with great improvement and advantage) are apt, when they return to their study after half-an-hour's absence, to forget where they left off."

He cites the authority of "great antiquity" for these divisions, Homer having divided "his great work" [*The Iliad*] into twenty-four books and "hawked them all separately," Virgil giving us his poem in twelve books, and "our Milton" originally publishing *Paradise Lost* in ten books, "till, being puffed up by the praise of his friends, he put himself on the same footing with the Roman poet." He concludes that "it becomes an author generally to divide a book, as it does a butcher to joint his meat, for such assistance is of great help to both the reader and the carver."

These remarks were something new in English fiction. Other authors may have divided their novels into books and chapters with descriptive titles, but none had made such careful divisions as Fielding, nor taken the trouble to explain their purpose. The introductory chapters and facetious chapter headings are to be found in Scarron, and the division into books is undoubtedly influenced by the classics. Though he seems only half serious, Fielding's reasons for the divisions of his novel are highly sensible.

In Book III, Chapter I, Matter Prefatory in Praise of Biography, he contrasts historians who record external facts with biographers, holding that "It is most certain that truth is to be found only in the works of those who celebrate the lives of great men, and are commonly called biographers." Historians can satisfactorily "describe countries and cities, . . . but as to the actions and characters of men, their writings are not quite so authentic." They differ widely as to facts of human nature, though they may agree as to facts of time and place. Biographers, however, are different; "the facts we deliver may be relied on, though we often mistake the age and country wherein they happened." He mentions such mistakes of external fact in *Don Quixote*, *Gil Blas*, *Le Roman Comique*, *The Arabian Nights*, *The History of Marianne*, and *Le Paysan Parvenu*, whose authors "are contented to copy nature," and asks:

Is not such a book as that which records the achievements of the renowned Don Quixote more worthy the name of a history than even Mariana's: for, whereas the latter is confined to a particular period of time, and to a particular nation, the former is the history of the world in general, at least that part which is polished by laws, arts, and sciences; and of that from the time it was first polished to this day; nay, and forwards as long as it shall so remain?[1]

Applying these observations to *Joseph Andrews*, Fielding says, "I describe not men, but manners; not an individual, but a species." His characters, nevertheless, are taken from life, and, he says, "I have writ little more than I have seen." He does not mean to libel particular persons in his story, but as to his hard-hearted lawyer in the stage-coach, he says, "When the first mean selfish creature appeared on the human stage, who made self the center of the whole creation, who would give himself no pain, incur no danger, advance no money, to assist or preserve his fellow-creatures; then was our lawyer born; and while such a person as I have described exists on earth, so long shall he remain upon it." The purpose of such character portrayal is "not to expose one pitiful wretch to the small and contemptible circle of his acquaintance; but to hold the glass to thousands in their closets, that they may contemplate their deformity, and endeavour to reduce it, and thus by suffering private mortification may avoid public shame." This purpose, he insists, distinguishes the satirist from the libeler, "for the former privately corrects the fault for the benefit of the person, like a parent; the latter publickly exposes the person himself, as an example to others, like an executioner."

Mrs. Tow-wouse, though quite different in circumstance, strongly resembles the lawyer, he remarks, and might even be found upon a throne at some time, though at present she stands behind the bar at an inn. "In short, where extreme turbulency of temper, avarice, and an insensibility of human misery, with a degree of hypocrisy, have united in a female composition, Mrs. Tow-wouse was that woman; and where a good inclination, eclipsed by a poverty of spirit and understanding, hath glimmered

[1] Fielding may here have in mind the dictum of Aristotle, that poetry is more serious and philosophical than mere factual history.

forth in a man that man hath been no other than her sneaking husband."

Fielding then leaves his reader with one caution "more of an opposite kind: for, as in most of our particular characters we mean not to lash individuals, but all of the like sort, so, in our general descriptions, we mean not universals, but would be understood with many exceptions." In his satirical and condemnatory descriptions of the great, for instance, he does not mean to include those who combine greatness of mind and character with greatness of position, such as his friends Lord Lyttleton and Ralph Allen, whom he clearly indicates, but only "a set of wretches, who, while they are a disgrace to their ancestors, whose honours and fortunes they inherit (or perhaps a greater to their mother, for such degeneracy is scarce credible), have the insolence to treat those with disregard who are at least equal to the founders of their own splendour

These statements develop further the realistic and satirical theories of the Author's Preface. Fielding calls himself a biographer, not in the particular sense, but as one who truly portrays human character His realism in character is not merely external, but it is truth to the abiding traits and instincts of man. He reminds us again of his moral purpose, to be accomplished by means of satire, and not libel, by exposing to each man privately the vices he may share with the lawyer and Mrs. Tow-wouse, or his vicious noblemen. In proposing to portray types of human character he acknowledges his debt to the character sketch of the seventeenth century and the character essays of Addison and Steele.

III

THE THEORY OF TOM JONES

FIELDING develops his initial chapters more carefully and at more regular intervals in *Tom Jones* than in *Joseph Andrews*. In his conception of the novel these introductory chapters are like the chorus of the drama interpreting the meaning of the passing incidents, or they are monologues and asides of the author turned player when he wishes to take the audience into his confidence.

Book I, Chapter I, The Introduction to the Work, or Bill of Fare to the Feast, opens with a characteristically humorous figure, recalling the comparison of the book divisions and chapter titles in *Joseph Andrews* to inns. "An author ought to consider himself, not as a gentleman who gives a private or eleemosynary treat, but rather as one who keeps a public ordinary, at which all persons are welcome for their money." The keeper of an ordinary, being bound to please his customers and avoid giving offense, should allow them to choose their own fare by providing "a bill of fare which all persons may peruse at their first entrance into the house; and having thence acquainted themselves with the entertainment which they may expect, may either stay and regale with what is provided for them, or may depart to some other ordinary better accommodated to their taste." Fielding professes to take the hint from these "honest victuallers" in prefixing "not only a general bill of fare to our whole entertainment," but likewise giving the reader "particular bills to every course which is to be served up in this and the ensuing volumes."

The "bill of fare" follows: "The provision, then, which we have here made is no other than *Human Nature*." Nor need the reader fear monotony in his diet, for "in human nature, though here collected under one general name, is such prodigious variety, that a cook will have sooner gone through all the species of animal and vegetable food in the world, than an author will be able to exhaust so extensive a subject." To the objection "apprehended from the more delicate, that this dish is too common and vulgar," Fielding replies: "Many exquisite viands might be rejected by the epicure, if it was a sufficient cause for his contemning of them as common and vulgar, that something was to be found in the most paltry alleys under the same name. In reality, true nature is as difficult to be met with in authors, as the Bayonne ham, or Bologna sausage, is to be found in the shops." The whole "consists in the cookery of the author," he says, quoting Pope's couplet,

> "True wit is nature to advantage drest;
> What oft was thought, but ne'er so well exprest."

The only difference between the food of the nobleman and the porter, "if both are at dinner on the same ox or calf," lies "in the seasoning, the dressing, the garnishing, and the setting forth. Hence the one provokes and incites the most languid appetite, and the other turns and palls that which is the sharpest and keenest."

In books, then, "the excellence of the mental entertainment consists less in the subject than in the author's skill in well dressing it up." In this he professes to have adhered closely to one of the highest principles of the best cook of the age, in setting first plain and then fancy dishes before his guests. "In like manner we shall represent human nature at first to the keen appetite of our reader, in that more plain and simple manner in which it is found in the country, and shall hereafter hash and ragoo it with all the high French and Italian seasoning of affectation and vice which courts and cities afford." By this means he hopes to make his reader desirous of reading on forever, just as the great cook mentioned made his guests wish to eat forever.

This chapter, although facetious, is interesting for two reasons. The first is Fielding's comment, expressed in the figure of the keeper of the ordinary, on the position of the novelist in relation to his reader. He feels that the novelist should give his reader some accurate indication of the contents of his whole novel and of its subdivisions. He himself does this admirably, although his chapter headings are sometimes ironic or facetious. This custom has been largely abandoned in the recent novel, but has been followed, partly from the example of Fielding, by such great novelists as Scott, Dickens, Thackeray, and Hardy. The latter two especially recall Fielding in their titles. The second point of interest in this chapter is the announcement, at the outset, of Fielding's realistic purpose in *Tom Jones*. Human nature in all its variety is to be his subject, presented first in plain and simple country life, and later in the vice and affectation of city life This is in harmony with the comic epic theory expressed in *Joseph Andrews*, which proposed to follow nature and present scenes of low life as well as high. The quotation of Pope's couplet and Fielding's comment on it indicate Fielding's method of judging a novel. Not the subject, but the author's skill in treating it, in giving it artistic form, just sentiments, and appropriate diction, should finally determine a novel's worth. Most intelligent critics have applied a similar test to the novel, since Fielding raised it to the level of high art.

In concluding Book I, Chapter II, Fielding tells his reader, "I intend to digress through this whole history, as often as I see occasion, of which I am myself a better judge than any pitiful critic whatever." He assumes that it is the author's privilege to intrude on the story at his pleasure, and to comment on his characters or their situations. This shows the influence of the character essay, for Addison and Steele were accustomed to comment on their characters. Fielding was a natural essayist, as his periodical writings and novels show, and could not resist digressive comment. Many novelists since him, particularly Thackeray, have adopted this custom with delightful results. The asides in *Vanity Fair* strongly recall those in *Tom Jones*.

In Book II, Chapter I, Showing What Kind of a History This Is; What It is Like, and What It is Not Like, Fielding discusses his theory of "history," as the term is used in the title, *The*

History of Tom Jones: a Foundling. Though this work is called a history, and not a life, he says, "yet we intend in it rather to pursue the method of those writers, who profess to disclose the revolutions of countries, than to imitate the painful and voluminous historian, who, to preserve the regularity of his series, thinks himself obliged to fill up as much paper with the detail of months and years in which nothing remarkable happened, as he employs upon those notable eras when the greatest scenes have been transacted on the human stage." Fielding proposes that "When any extraordinary scene presents itself (as we trust will often be the case), we shall spare no pains nor paper to open it at large to our reader; but if whole years should pass without producing anything worthy his notice, we shall not be afraid of a chasm in our history; but shall hasten on to matters of consequence, and leave such periods of time totally unobserved."

As a result of this selective method, "My reader . . . is not to be surprised, if, in the course of this work, he shall find some chapters very short, and others altogether as long; some that contain only the time of a single day, and others that comprise years; in a word, if my history sometimes seems to stand still, and sometimes to fly." And again he assumes the freedom of the innovator: "For all which I shall not look on myself as accountable to any court of critical jurisdiction whatever: for as I am, in reality, the founder of a new province of writing, so I am at liberty to make what laws I please therein. And these laws, my readers, whom I consider as my subjects, are bound to believe in and to obey; with which that they may readily and cheerfully comply, I do hereby assure them that I shall principally regard their ease and advantage in all such institutions."

Fielding's use of the term "history" indicates the lack, in his day, of fixed boundaries between literary forms, and the consequent various uses of such terms. What he means by "history" we should call "fictitious biography." The term was commonly used in this sense in the eighteenth century, as in Smollett's *History of an Atom*, or the popular *History of a Guinea*. It carries with it the implication of verisimilitude, to distinguish such writings from the fantastic romances. There is doubtless a little burlesque and irony in Fielding's use of the term, in ridicule of the many eighteenth century writers who used it to give their work dignity and apparent truth. He gives the term added significance by his distinction between the two sorts of political history, the selective and the inclusive, the former of which he proposes to imitate. In this he is making a conscious advance in technique over his predecessors and contemporaries, particularly over Defoe and Richardson. They, of necessity, used some degree of selection, but their novels contain too much narration of insignificant events, having no bearing on the main action of the story. The letters of Pamela and Clarissa are especially to blame in this, although their minute detail occasionally adds vividness to the story. Fielding, like the best novelists after him, realized the advantages of careful selection of significant actions, to preserve the unity of character and action, and to give the story swiftness of movement. He omits long periods of time in which nothing happens material to his central purpose, which is to create character by revealing typical actions. This principle was an important contribution to the theory of the novel.

In Book IV, Chapter I, Containing Five Pages of Paper, Fielding distinguishes his novels from factual histories.

> As truth distinguishes our writings from those idle romances which are filled with monsters, the productions, not of nature, but of distempered brains; and which have therefore been recommended by an eminent critic to the sole use of the pastry-cook; so, on the other hand, we would avoid any resemblance to that kind of history which a celebrated poet seems to think is no less calculated for the emolument of the brewer, as the reading it should always be attended with a tankard of good ale.

The difference is to lie in the use of poetic ornament, by the example of Homer.

> That our work, therefore, might be in no danger of being likened to the labours of these historians, we have taken every occasion of interspersing through the whole sundry similes, descriptions, and other kind of poetical embellishments. These

are, indeed, designed to supply the place of the said ale, and to refresh the mind, whenever those slumbers, which in a long work are apt to invade the reader as well as the writer, shall begin to creep upon him.[1] Without interruptions of this kind, the best narrative of plain matter-of-fact must overpower every reader; for nothing but the everlasting watchfulness, which Homer hath ascribed to Jove himself, can be proof against a newspaper of many volumes.

He leaves to the reader the judgment of how appropriately these ornaments are used. At this point in the story the occasion for poetic ornament is the introduction of "the heroine of this heroic, historical, prosaic poem." For this device he facetiously pleads the precedents of "our tragic poets, who seldom fail to prepare their audience for the reception of their principal characters," by appropriate music, and the managers of playhouses, who send on a procession to introduce their heroes.

The citation of these latter precedents is obviously ironic. Fielding regards their use of such devices as ridiculous, but he himself sometimes seriously attempts to achieve poetic beauty by them. At other times he burlesques them, but occasionally, as in the introduction of Sophia which follows this chapter, he reaches poetic heights. In the hands of such masters of style as Scott, Thackeray, and Hardy the introduction of these purple passages has added poetry to the novel. None of Fielding's predecessors or contemporaries in the novel had sufficiently fine styles to vie with him in introducing "poetical embellishments."

Fielding talks amusingly of his introductory chapters in Book V, Chapter I, Of the Serious in Writing, and for What Purpose It is Introduced.

Peradventure there may be no parts in this prodigious work which will give the reader less pleasure in the perusing, than those which have given the author the greatest pains in composing. Among these probably may be reckoned those initial essays which we have prefixed to the historical matter contained in every book; and which we have determined to be essentially necessary, to this kind of writing, of which we have set ourselves at the head.

[1] This statement is probably a hit at Richardson.

He does not consider himself bound to give any reason for this, "it being abundantly sufficient that we have laid it down as a rule necessary to be observed in all prosai-comi-epic writing." He ironically supports this position by citing the classical unities of time and place, established by the critics as essential to dramatic poetry, for which they give no reason but ancient authority. Also, he says, the word "low," as used by modern dramatic critics, has never been satisfactorily explained. "In such cases, therefore, we are apt to conclude there are sound and good reasons at the bottom, though we are unfortunately not able to see so far."

He then reveals his scorn for most of the critics. "Now, in reality, the world have paid too great a compliment to critics, and have imagined them men of much greater profundity than they really are. From this complacence, the critics have been emboldened to assume a dictatorial power, and have so far succeeded, that they are now become masters, and have the assurance to give laws to those authors from whose predecessors they originally received them." In his conception, "the critic, rightly considered, is no more than the clerk, whose office it is to transcribe the rules and laws laid down by those great judges whose vast strength hath placed them in the light of legislators, in the several sciences over which they presided." This was the position of the ancient critics, but "in process of time, and in ages of ignorance, the clerk began to invade the power and assume the dignity of his master." Out of this change in position arose "an obvious, and perhaps an unavoidable error; these critics, being men of shallow capacities, very easily mistook mere form for substance. . . Little circumstances, which were perhaps accidental in a great author, were by these critics considered to constitute his chief merit, and transmitted as essentials to be observed by all his successors." Thus "many rules for good writing have been established, which have not the least foundation in truth or nature; and which commonly serve for no other purpose than to curb and restrain genius, in the same manner as it would have restrained the dancing-master, had the many excellent treaties on that art laid it down as an essential rule that every man must dance in chains."

What better criticism could be made of the critics who dominated English criticism in the seventeenth and eighteenth centuries? They drew their rules, not directly from great authors, but from the ancient critics, Aristotle and Horace being their greatest authorities. Fielding respected these ancient critics, but not their modern imitators. He felt that it was genius, and not the critic, which really set the standard, and having a share of genius himself, he made his own rules, though often guided in making them by previous examples.

To avoid being thought too dogmatic, Fielding gives his reason for interspersing "these several digressive essays in the course of this work." They are introduced upon the principle of contrast, "which runs through all the works of the creation, and may probably have a large share in constituting in us the idea of all beauty, as well natural as artificial: for what demonstrates the beauty and excellence of anything but its reverse?" He gives several examples of contrast, some serious, some facetious, such as its use in English pantomime, in which the "duller part," the comic element, is set off by the "dullest part," the serious element which precedes it. His greatest precedent in the use of contrast is Homer, who occasionally introduces comparatively dull parts in order to set off the more stirring scenes which follow. "To say the truth, these soporific parts are so many scenes of serious artfully interwoven, in order to contrast and set off the rest; and this is the true meaning of a late facetious writer, who told the public that whenever he was dull they might be assured there was a design in it." He professes to be laboriously dull in these introductory chapters in order to set off the brightness of his story.

Though facetiously expressed, this is a sound reason for the inclusion of the initial essays. Besides stating his theory of the novel and displaying his delightful humor, they surely serve to vary the monotony of the long story and, though never dull or over-serious, to contrast in subject-matter and tone with the narrative. Many novelists since Fielding have used such digressions; so the device is another important contribution to the theory of the novel. Thackeray, Fielding's closest imitator, has, in *Vanity Fair*, made the best use of these essay-like passages.

Interesting comment on the dramatic element in Fielding's conception of the novel appears in Book VII, Chapter I, A Comparison between the World and the Stage. "The world hath been often compared to the theatre; and many grave writers, as well as the poets, have considered human life as a great drama, resembling in almost every particular, those scenical representations which Thespis is first reported to have invented, and which have been since received with so much approbation and delight in all polite countries." This comparison has become so common "that some words proper to the theatre, and which were at first metaphorically applied to the world, are now indiscriminately and literally spoken of both." Such words as "stage" and "scene" are applied generally to both life and the stage. He does not account for it by the desire of the public to compliment the playwrights or actors who have so well imitated life, for the public is more fond of hissing and buffeting them. The real reasons are, first, that "some have considered the larger part of mankind in the light of actors, as personating characters no more their own, and to which in fact they have no better title, than the player hath to be in earnest thought the king or emperor whom he represents. Thus the hypocrite may be said to be a player; and indeed the Greeks called them both by one and the same name." The second reason for this comparison is the brevity both of life and of plays.

In all these comparisons, however, "the resemblance hath been always taken from the stage only," and no one has considered the audience at the drama of life. "But as nature often exhibits some of her best performances to a very full house, so will the behavior of her spectators no less admit the abovementioned comparison than that of her actors. In this vast theatre of time are seated the friend and the critic; here are claps and shouts, hisses and groans; in short everything which was ever seen or heard at the Theatre-Royal." He imagines the attitude of the various parts of the audience during the incident where Black George runs away with Tom's £500. "Those who sat in the world's upper gallery treated that incident, I am well convinced, with their usual vociferation; and every term of scurrilous reproach was most probably vented on that occasion." Descending to the next order of spectators, "we should have found an equal degree of abhorrence, though less of noise and scurrility." The pit was divided in its opinion as usual; some objected to the producing of such villany without punishing it severely, some of the author's friends cried out, "Look'ee, gentlemen, the man is a villain, but it is nature for all that," and all the young critics, "the clerks, apprentices, etc., called it low and fell a groaning." The boxes behaved with customary politeness, most of them not attending to the performance, a few saying Black George was "a bad kind of man; while others refused to give their opinion, till they had heard that of the best judges."

Fielding then describes his own attitude toward his characters.

Now we, who are admitted behind the scenes of this great theatre of Nature (and no author ought to write anything besides dictionaries and spelling-books who hath not this privilege), can censure the action, without conceiving any absolute detestation of the person whom perhaps Nature may not have designed to act an ill part in all her dramas; for in this instance life most exactly resembles the stage, since it is often the same person who represents the villain and the hero; and he who engages your admiration to-day will probably attract your contempt to-morrow.

Garrick, usually the tragic hero, sometimes played the fool, as, though in jest only, did Scipio the Great, and Laelius the Wise, according to Horace. "But several eminent characters have, in numberless instances of their lives, played the fool egregiously in earnest; so far as to render it a matter of some doubt whether their wisdom or folly was predominant; or whether they were better entitled to the applause or censure, the admiration or contempt, the love or hatred, of mankind."

Those who are acquainted with the disguises assumed in this great theatre, and with the "fantastic and capricious behaviour of the Passions, who are the managers and directors," learn to understand the *nil admirari* of Horace. Reason, the patentee of the theatre, is said to be "a very idle fellow" who seldom exerts himself. "A single bad act no more constitutes a villain in life, than a single bad part on the stage. The passions, like the managers of a play-house, often force men upon parts without consulting their judgment, and sometimes without regard to their talents." For these reasons, Fielding concludes, "the man of candour and of true understanding is never hasty to condemn," and can "censure an imperfection, or even a vice, without rage against the guilty party."

Fielding's experience in writing plays and his long association with the theatre, as well as his familiarity with the classical drama and its critics, made it natural for him to adopt this dramatic conception of life and of the novel. He could most easily think, as Shakespeare did, of the world he portrayed as a great stage,

> And all the men and women merely players.

Not only do his novels have dramatic form, in plot construction and character portrayal, but Fielding thinks of himself as the playwright, manipulating his players, with his eye constantly on the audience and its reactions. This dramatic conception of the novel helped to establish the important convention that the novelist, like the playwright, is assumed to be omniscient. Most of the great novelists since Fielding have adopted the omniscient method, while before him the point of view method prevailed. Defoe tells his stories through the mouths of his characters, as do Swift, Lesage, and Richardson. The novel owes mainly to Fielding this new point of view, the attitude of the playwright toward his play. Thackeray follows Fielding's method very closely in *Vanity Fair*. He conceives of his story as a puppet-show, the characters being the puppets, of which he is the creator and manipulator.

The attitude toward his characters expressed in this chapter reveals Fielding's tolerant wisdom. He sees that few persons are completely and always bad, that we should condemn the act and not the person. Considering how much the passions, plus time and chance, control man's actions upon the stage of life, he is never "hasty to condemn." This attitude enables him to satirize human folly and weakness without bitterness or loss of sympathy.

Book VIII, Chapter I, A Wonderful Long Chapter Concerning the Marvellous; Being Much the Longest of All Our Introductory Chapters, adds some significant features to Fielding's conception of realism. As the ensuing book is to contain some matters "of a more strange and surprizing kind" than any previous one, he thinks it appropriate to speak "of that species of writing which is called the marvellous." Because of the wide diversity of opinion concerning it, he proposes to set some bounds to the marvelous.

His first rule is that "it may very reasonably be required of every writer, that he keeps within the bounds of possibility; and still remembers that what it is not possible for man to perform, it is scarce possible for man to believe he did perform." He disapproves of the excessive use of supernatural beings by the ancients, though he confesses that their readers may have believed in such beings, and wishes "Homer could have known the rule prescribed by Horace, to introduce supernatural agents as seldom as possible." A Christian writer cannot use any of his own deities, nor can he wisely use heathen deities who are no longer credited. "The only supernatural agents which can in any manner be allowed to us moderns, are ghosts; but of these I would advise an author to be extremely sparing." He advises against any use of ghosts if "a horse-laugh in the reader would be any great prejudice or mortification" to the author. The use of elves and fairies is also condemned. "Man therefore is the highest subject (unless on very extraordinary occasions indeed) which presents itself to the pen of our historian, or of our poet; and in relating his actions, great care is to be taken that we do not exceed the capacity of the agent we describe."

In addition to this, moreover, "We must keep likewise within the rules of probability." He cites an opinion of Aristotle or "some wise man whose authority will be as weighty when it is as old, 'That it is no excuse for a poet who relates what is incredible, that the thing related is really matter of fact'." He thinks this true for the poet, but doubts its applicability to the public historian, who is "obliged to record matters as he finds them, though they be of such extraordinary a nature as will require no small degree of historical faith to swallow them." Such facts he is justified in recording if they occur in the thread of the story and constitute essential parts of it. "But there are other facts not of such consequence nor so necessary, which, though ever so well attested, may nevertheless be sacrificed to oblivion in complacence to the scepticism of a reader." If the historian confines himself to what really happened, "he will sometimes fall into the marvellous, but never into the incredible."

In private history (the novel), however, there is greater reason for not deserting probability. The historians who relate public transactions, being supported by common notoriety and public records, have the advantage over those who confine themselves to scenes of private life. "We who deal in private character, who search into the most retired recesses, and draw forth examples of virtue and vice from holes and corners of the world, are in a more dangerous situation. As we have no public notoriety, no concurrent testimony, no records to support and corroborate what we deliver, it becomes us to keep within the limits not only of possibility, but of probability too; and this more especially in painting what is greatly good and amiable." Men will readily believe in exorbitant knavery and folly, because the ill-nature of men "adds great support and strength to faith." But people are loath to believe in such perfectly good and noble men as his generous friend Ralph Allen.

His next rule follows logically and is drawn from the drama, being, "what the dramatic critics call conservation of character; and it requires a very extraordinary degree of judgment, and a most exact knowledge of human nature." Not only should the actions be "within the compass of human agency, and which human agents may probably be supposed to do; but they should be likely for the very actors and characters themselves to have performed; for what may be only wonderful and surprizing in one man, may become improbable, or indeed impossible, when related of another." He adds "that for a man to act in direct contradiction to the dictates of his nature, is, if not impossible, as improbable and as miraculous as anything which can well be conceived." A man's extraordinary acts, if in character, constitute the truly marvelous, but if ascribed to a different character they would be incredible. He notes that "Our modern authors of comedy have fallen almost universally into the error here hinted at; their heroes generally are notoriously rogues, and their heroines abandoned jades, during the first four acts; but in the fifth, the former become very worthy gentlemen, and the latter women of virtue and discretion; nor is the writer often so kind as to give himself the least trouble to reconcile or account for this monstrous change and incongruity."

Within the rules he has laid down, Fielding concludes, "every writer may be permitted to deal as much in the wonderful as he pleases; nay, if he thus keeps within the rules of credibility, the more he can surprize the reader, the more he will engage his attention, and the more he will charm him. He quotes the fifth chapter of Pope's *Bathos* to the effect that "The great art of all poetry is to mix truth with fiction, in order to join the credible with the surprizing."[1] For though an author should remain within the probable, "it is by no means necessary that his characters, or his incidents, should be trite, common, or vulgar; such as happen in every street, or in every house, or which may be met with in the home articles of a newspaper. Nor must he be inhibited from showing many persons and things, which may possibly have never fallen within the knowledge of great part of his readers." If the writer observes the rules here set down, "he hath discharged his part; and is then entitled to some faith from

[1] Fielding uses this dictum seriously, while Pope uses it ironically, to ridicule the absurdities to which the misuse of this rule carries the practitioners of bathos. Pope says further: "Our author shall produce the credible, by painting Nature in her lowest simplicity; and the surprizing, by contradicting common opinion. In the very manners he will affect the marvelous; he will draw Achilles with the patience of Job; a Prince talking like a Jack-pudding; a maid of honour selling bargains; a footman speaking like a philosopher; and a fine gentleman like a scholar."

his reader, who is indeed guilty of critical infidelity if he disbelieves him."

This is the earliest statement by a great novelist of the rules of credibility, which have been carefully followed by all true novelists. The novel being, as we understand it, a realistic picture of actual life, this rule is essential to it. Any prose fiction which does not remain within the realm of probability in the actions of its characters is not a novel but a romance. Our conception of the romance allows of the introduction of the fantastic, the improbable idealization of acts and characters, and the free use of superhuman or supernatural elements, but our conception of the novel, for which Fielding laid the basis, does not.

Book IX, Chapter I, Of Those Who Lawfully May, and of Those Who May Not, Write Such Histories as This, contains another reason for the inclusion of the introductory chapters and a description of the qualities requisite to the novelist. Fielding says he uses the introductory chapters "as a kind of mark or stamp, which may hereafter enable a very indifferent reader to distinguish what is true and genuine in this historic kind of writing, from what is false and counterfeit." Such a mark is the more necessary, he says, because of the recent successes of two or three novelists, which will probably call forth a swarm of imitators. Just as Addison used Greek and Latin mottoes at the head of *The Spectator* papers, Fielding uses these preliminary essays to guard against imitation, for just as no one could imitate the titles in *The Spectator* without a knowledge of the learned languages, so by writing these essays Fielding secured himself "from the imitation of those who are utterly incapable of any degree of reflection, and whose learning is not equal to an essay."

Most writers of novels and romances, he says, through lack of ability have caused an almost universal contempt for "all historical writers who do not draw their materials from records." More ignorant and stupid people have written novels and romances than have written any other kind of writing, seeming to think that for "the composition of novels and romances, nothing is necessary but paper, pens, and ink, with the manual capacity of using them." He has avoided calling his novel a "romance" in order to escape the contempt of the world. He wishes to prevent imitation not only to avoid bringing dishonor "on one of the most useful as well as entertaining of all kinds of writing," but also to prevent positive moral detriment, through reading bad novels, to "the characters of many good and valuable members of society."

To prevent these abuses "of leisure, of letters, and of the liberty of the press," Fielding states some qualifications, "every one of which are in a pretty high degree necessary to this order of historians." The first is genius, "without a full vein of which no study, says Horace, can avail us." Genius is "that power or rather those powers of the mind, which are capable of penetrating into all things within our reach and knowledge, and of distinguishing their essential differences." Those powers are invention and judgment, and both are "called by the collective name of genius, as they are of those gifts of nature which we bring with us into the world." Invention is not a creative faculty, which most romance writers may claim, but "discovery or finding out; or to explain it at large, a quick and sagacious penetration into the true essence of all objects of our contemplation." This can rarely exist "without the concomitancy of judgment; for how we can be said to have discovered the true essence of two things, without discerning their difference seems to me hard to conceive." In spite of a wide opinion to the contrary these two powers, he affirms, are almost always found together.

Learning is the second requirement, for "tools are of no service to a workman, when they are not sharpened by art, or when he wants rules to direct him in his work, or hath no matter to work upon." Learning supplies art, rules, and matter. "Nature can only furnish us with capacity; or, as I have chose to illustrate it, with the tools of our profession; learning must fit them for use, must direct them in it, and, lastly, must contribute part at least of the materials. A competent knowledge of history and of the belles-lettres is here absolutely necessary; and without this share of knowledge at least, to affect the character of an historian, is as vain as to endeavour at building a house without timber or mortar, or brick or stone."

The third requisite is experience, or "conversation." "So necessary is this to the understanding the characters of men, that none are more ignorant of them than those learned pedants whose lives have been entirely consumed in colleges, and among books, for however exquisitely human nature may have been described by writers, the true practical system can be learnt only in the world." Experience is necessary to perfect oneself in any art or occupation. This should be universal, "that is, with all ranks and degrees of men; for the knowledge of what is called high life will not instruct him in low; nor *è converso*, will his being acquainted with the inferior part of mankind teach him the manners of the superior." To know and write about one class is insufficient, "for the follies of either rank do in reality illustrate each other. For instance, the affectation of high life appears more glaring and ridiculous from the simplicity of the low; and again, the rudeness and barbarity of this latter, strikes with much stronger ideas of absurdity, when contrasted with, and opposed to, the politeness which controls the former." The historian will benefit by both these "conversations," finding examples of plainness, honesty, and sincerity in the lower classes, and in the higher, refinement, elegance, and a liberality of spirit, "which last quality I myself have scarce ever seen in men of low birth and education."

These three qualities will not avail the novelist "unless he have what is generally meant by a good heart, and be capable of feeling." In order to portray deep distress a man must feel it, and similarly, "I am convinced I never make my reader laugh heartily but where I have laughed before him; unless it should happen at any time, that instead of laughing with me he should be inclined to laugh at me."

Fielding is more serious here than in most of the introductory chapters. He is trying to set high standards for the novelist and to discourage ignorant and unqualified imitators. His scorn for the popular novels and romances of his time makes him desire to be classed above them. His standards indicate both his idealism and his common sense. His conception of genius is rational and pragmatic; it is the ability to understand human life completely and to recognize the essential differences between objects. This is a much more comprehensible and satisfying definition than the usual romantic one. His own experience showed him the value of wide reading in the classics and moderns for acquiring the theory and the materials for his novels. Without familiarity with literary forms and materials, he realized, talent alone is nothing. Like Fielding, the greatest English novelists, except Dickens, have been men of broad learning.

Fielding had the wide experience of life prescribed for the novelist, which qualified him to be the first great realist in the novel. The great novelists have all been men of wide experience. The novel has become the best medium of expression for mature and seasoned writers like Dickens, Thackeray, Hardy, Conrad, and Galsworthy.

The setting of these standards again shows Fielding's consciousness of innovation. His importance as a theorist appears when we consider that they are still the basic requirements of the novelist's art. In enunciating them Fielding set the writing of fiction upon a new and higher plane.

Book X, Chapter I, Containing Instructions Very Necessary to be Perused by Modern Critics, warns critics against hastily condemning any incidents or characters in the novel. "This work may, indeed, be considered as a great creation of our own; and for a little reptile of a critic to presume to find fault with any of its parts, without knowing the manner in which the whole is connected, and before he comes to the final catastrophe, is a most presumptuous absurdity." He should not "find out too near a resemblance between certain characters here introduced"; for instance between two landladies who appear, because "there are certain characteristics in which most individuals of every profession and occupation agree. . . To preserve these characteristics, and at the same time to diversify their operations, is one talent of a good writer."[1] Another such talent is to "mark the nice distinction between two persons actuated by the same vice or folly; and as this last talent is found in very few writers, so is the true discernment of it found in as few readers."

His next warning is "not to condemn a character as a bad one, because it is not perfectly a good one." If the reader delights in them, these models of perfection may be found in many books; "but, as we have not, in the course of our conversation, ever happened to meet with any such person, we have not chosen to introduce any such here." He doubts whether a perfectly good or entirely bad man ever existed; nor can he

> conceive the good purposes served by inserting characters of such angelic perfection, or such diabolical depravity, in any work of invention; since, from contemplating either, the mind of man is more likely to be overwhelmed with sorrow and shame than to draw any good uses from such patterns; for in the former instance he may be both concerned and ashamed to see a pattern of excellence in his nature, which he may reasonably despair of ever arriving at; and in contemplating the latter he may be no less affected with those uneasy sensations, at seeing the nature of which he is a partaker degraded into so odious and detestable a creature.

On the other hand Fielding sees an advantage in presenting characters containing enough goodness "to engage the admiration and affection of a well-disposed mind," with enough blemishes to "raise our compassion rather than our abhorrence." These are morally beneficial to the reader, since "the foibles and vices of men, in whom there is great mixture of good, become more glaring objects from the virtues which contrast them and show their deformity; and when we find such vices attended with their evil consequence to our favorite characters, we are not only taught to shun them for our own sake, but to hate them for the mischiefs they have already brought on those we love."

[1] Macaulay, in his essay on Madame d' Arblay, calls this "differentiation of characters," commenting on Jane Austen's ability to make four clergymen in similar circumstances distinct persons. Perhaps Macaulay was partially indebted to Fielding for this theory.

Besides showing Fielding's impatience with captious and ignorant critics, this chapter justifies the realistic method of character portrayal. Characters of "angelic perfection," as drawn by Richardson in *Pamela, Clarissa,* and *Sir Charles Grandison,* Fielding regarded as depressing, rather than inspiring. On the other hand, such diabolical characters as Lovelace or the heroes of the criminal pamphlets must disgust us by their depravity. Fielding seems right, then, in presenting average persons, combining virtues and vices in their composition, as they are artistically more effective, because more real, and morally more beneficial, because they attract our sympathies.

Book XI, Chapter I, A Crust for the Critics, eloquently expresses Fielding's opinions of unfair criticism. He ironically describes critics as judges who only condemn, and seriously calls them slanderers who ruin without any justification the reputations of authors. His hatred is so intense that he speaks of them as "abject slaves" and "odious vermin," as "monsters" who murder with their slander. Books are the children of their authors and "may most truly be called the riches of their father; and many of them have with true filial piety fed their parent in his old age: so that not only the affection, but the interest, of the author may be highly injured by these slanderers whose poisonous breath brings his book to an untimely end." The slander of a book is really the slander of the author, for you cannot call a book "sad stuff, horrid nonsense, etc.," without calling the author a blockhead. To those who think he has not treated this subject "with decent solemnity," he says, "surely a man may speak truth with a smiling countenance." His serious opinion is that "to depreciate a book maliciously, or even wantonly, is at least a very ill-natured office; and a morose, snarling critic may, I believe, be suspected to be a bad man."

Fielding's sensitiveness to unfair criticism is easily understood, for his own writings, notably *Joseph Andrews,* had suffered by it. This chapter may be taken as Fielding's rebuke to those who had damned his first novel, the political and literary enemies made through his satirical plays and essays, as well as through *Joseph Andrews* itself.

In Book XII, Chapter I, Showing What is to be Deemed Plagiarism in a Modern Author, and What is to be Considered Lawful Prize, Fielding justifies his practice of quoting the ancient classics without acknowledgment. "The antients may be considered as a rich common, where every person who hath the smallest tenement in Parnassus hath a free right to fatten his muse." Or, he continues ironically, it may be considered that "we moderns are to the antients what the poor are to the rich" in England, where the poor neighbors of the squire regard his property as common spoil. But we moderns should "maintain the same strict honesty among ourselves which the mob show to one another." In other words, modern authors should not steal from one another, and with characteristic honesty and fairness he proposes strictly to acknowledge every borrowing from his contemporaries.

In Book XIII, Chapter I, An Invocation, Fielding calls upon "fame" and "substance" to prompt him to write, and invokes the assistance of Genius, Humanity, Learning, and Experience, already listed as essential to the novelist, to direct his pen. The "fame" he desires is to be "read with honour" by those who never knew or saw him, and whom he should never know or see. He wishes for "substance" only to support his family. The "Genius" invoked is that of the great humorists, with whom he hopes to be ranked. "Come, thou that hast inspired thy Aristophanes, thy Lucian, thy Cervantes, thy Rabelais, thy Molière, thy Shakespeare, thy Swift, thy Marivaux, fill my pages with humour; till mankind learn the good-nature to laugh only at the follies of others, and the humility to grieve at their own." He was familiar with all these writers, some of whom, as earlier shown, had considerable influence on the theory of his art.

"Humanity," equivalent to the "good heart" required of the novelist, with its "tender sensations" will enable him to "swell the heart" of his readers "with tides of grief, joy, and benevolence." "Learning," which he had worshiped "in thy favourite fields, where the limpid, gently-rolling Thames washes thy Etonian banks," is urged to open its "Maeonian and Mantuan coffers," all its philosophic, poetic, and historical treasures, whether with Greek or Roman characters it has chosen to inscribe the ponderous chests. Last he calls upon "Experience, long conversant with the wise, the good, the learned, and the polite," and "with every type of character, from the minister at his levee, to the bailiff in his spunging-house; from the duchess at her drum, to the land-lady behind her bar."

This invocation in the classical manner and florid, rhapsodical style might seem too heavy and sentimental if there were not always a suggestion of mockery and burlesque about it. Fielding seems always to have in the back of his mind the purpose of burlesquing the poets and romancers who took such classical devices too seriously.

Book XIV, Chapter I, An Essay to Prove That an Author Will Write the Better for Having Some Knowledge of the Subject on Which he Writes, is a development and illustration of the rule that experience is necessary to the novelist. Fielding is speaking here of actual experience, or "conversation," with the kind of life depicted. The chapter is aimed particularly at those novelists, like Richardson, and those playwrights, like Cibber, who portray "high life" without any knowledge of it, save that gained from novels or plays. Ironically he says, "I require no more than that a man should have some little knowledge of the subject on which he treats. . . With this alone a writer may sometimes do tolerably well; and indeed, without this, all the other learning in the world will stand him in little stead." Then, coming to his point: "I am apt to conceive, that one reason why so many English writers have totally failed in describing the manners of upper life, may possibly be, that in reality they know nothing of it." Unfortunately, he says, this is a knowledge not in the power of many authors to arrive at. Books and the stage give us a very imperfect idea of it. The only qualifications which permit one to converse with "this higher order of mortals" are "either birth or fortune, or, what is equivalent to both, the honourable profession of a gamester." The great seldom write themselves, as they regard writing as a "bad trade" which is "generally entered upon by the poorer and lower sort." Consequently we have in the novel and on the stage "those strange monsters in lace and embroidery, in silks and brocades, with vast wigs and hoops, which are no more to be found in real life than the centaur, the chimera, or any other creature of mere fiction." He confesses, however, that the knowledge of upper life, "though very necessary for preventing mistakes," is of little use to comic writers, because the highest life is usually the dullest, being all form and affectation, the persons lacking in character and humor, their lives being mainly "vanity and servile imitation."

Richardson's *Pamela* (1740) and *Clarissa* (1745) had stirred Fielding's laughter by their clumsy attempts to portray "upper life," and this chapter is one result of his amusement. Having been born a gentleman and having mingled in polite circles all his life, Fielding had none of the illusions about fashionable life which Richardson, born and bred in a lower station, naturally had. He saw it with its mask off, and with his usual clear-eyed philosophical intelligence judged it a thing of vanity and frivolity. He is sincere in saying that it supplies few interesting and humorous incidents to the comic writer, for in his novels he lays most of the vivid and humorous action in lower life. He uses high life chiefly, as he told us in the first chapter of *Tom Jones*, for contrast and variety.

Fielding's moral outlook is revealed in Book XV, Chapter I, Too Short to Need a Preface. He comments on the doctrine taught by "a set of religious, or rather moral writers," that "virtue is the certain road to happiness, and vice to misery, in this world." His only objection to this "very wholesome and comfortable" doctrine is its falsity. He will concede its truth with regard to the prudential qualities, "those cardinal virtues, which like good housewives stay at home, and mind only the business of their own family." These lead to happiness, and he would call them wisdom rather than virtue, after the manner of "the antient Epicureans, who held this wisdom to constitute the chief good." But unselfish virtue, "a certain relative quality, which is always busying itself without-doors, and seems as much interested in pursuing the good of others as its own," leads not surely to human happiness, but all too often to "poverty and contempt, with all the mischiefs which back-biting, envy, and ingratitude, can bring on mankind. . . Nay, sometimes perhaps we shall be obliged to wait upon the said happiness to a jail; since many by the above virtue have brought themselves thither." There are so many exceptions to the above rule that "We choose to dispute the doctrine on which it is founded, which we don't apprehend to be Christian, which we are convinced is not true, and which is indeed destructive of one of the noblest arguments that reason alone can furnish for the belief of immortality." He prefers to believe that unselfish virtue is rewarded in the after-life.

This passage, recalling Thackeray's pessimistic moralizing in *Vanity Fair*, reveals both the realistic and the religious qualities of Fielding's moral outlook. With his clear vision of life he saw, like Thackeray, that there is no causal connection between virtue and earthly happiness, unless by virtue we mean merely the prudential qualities. This truth is best illustrated in the character of Tom Jones. Fielding's sincerely religious nature appears in the belief implied at the end of the chapter, that such Christian charity as Tom displayed should not look to earthly happiness as its reward.

Fielding is sharply distinguished by this moral outlook from Defoe and Richardson, who had preached in their novels the middle-class doctrine that if you are good you will be happy. His theory of the novel did not include the provision at the end of the story of earthly rewards for the Christian virtues of his characters. The conventional ending which gives wealth and honor to the hero as rewards for unselfish virtue is precluded by Fielding's belief. He gives his good characters happiness at the end of his novels, but not as compensation for their goodness. By prudence and good fortune alone he allows them to win earthly happiness.

Book XVI, Chapter I, Of Prologues, facetiously compares the introductory chapters to the prologues of contemporary drama. Like prologues, they are harder to write than the matter which follows. "I can with less pains write one of the books of this history than the prefatory chapter to each of them." Just as playwrights often curse the man who invented the prologue, so Fielding apprehends "some future historian (if any one shall do me the honour of imitating my manner) will, after much scratching his pate, bestow some good wishes on my memory, for having first established these several initial chapters." Just as the prologue, though it originally was part of the piece itself, now has very little connection with the drama before which it stands, so these initial chapters "may as properly be prefixed to any other book in this history as to that which they introduce, or indeed to any other history as to this." In spite of the suffering which authors will endure from the invention of these chapters, however, the reader will find sufficient emolument in them, just as the spectator long has done in the prologue.

The prologue "serves the critic for an opportunity to try his faculty of hissing, and to tune his cat-call to the best advantage"; similarly in these chapters he "will be always sure of meeting with something that may serve as a whetstone to his noble spirit; so that he may fall with a more hungry appetite for censure on the history itself." The author has taken care to fit these chapters for this purpose by interspersing "somewhat of the sour or acid kind, in order to sharpen and stimulate the said spirit of criticism." Another advantage of the prologue and these chapters is that they may easily be skipped, and as the spectator of the play may linger over his dinner to miss the prologue, so the reader will "have the advantage of beginning to read at the fourth or fifth page instead of the first, a matter by no means of trivial consequence to persons who read books with no other view than to say they have read them, a more general motive to reading than is commonly imagined." He omits mention of any further "emoluments" of both prologues and initial chapters "since it occurs to us that the principal merit of both the prologue and the preface is that they be short."

Although obviously facetious, this chapter indicates a genuine parallel and shows that Fielding wrote with one eye on the drama. Very few novelists have used initial chapters, perhaps because, as Fielding jokingly says, they are difficult to write. The talent of an essayist, which few novelists have possessed, is required to write them successfully. Thackeray, who used the device successfully, though not so regularly as Fielding, had this talent. An argument against these chapters is that they impair the unity of the action, but in the hands of an essayist they are effective. Fielding's remark is true, that many of these chapters are not strictly relevant to the action which follows, but that does not impair the interest either of the chapters themselves or of the story. Instead they serve, as he has told us, to contrast with and set off the story. The device was probably suggested by his custom of writing prologues to his plays, as well as by the example of Scarron. This custom became so habitual that it made natural the use of introductory chapters to his Books, each of which might be considered a separate play. If he had been merely a story-teller, instead of a dramatist, the practice probably would not have arisen.

Book XVII, Chapter I, Containing a Portion of Introductory Writing, expresses Fielding's determination to abide by his rules of credibility. Having brought his characters into a situation where tragedy seems inevitable, Fielding considers the difficulty of bringing them "out of their present anguish and distress," and making them finally happy, which, as a comic writer, he feels obliged to do. Abiding by his rules, however, he promises that he will not lend his hero any of "that supernatural assistance with which we are entrusted, upon condition that we use it only on very important occasions." If he does not find natural means of extricating himself from his distresses, "we will do no violence to the truth and dignity of history for his sake; for we had rather relate that he was hanged at Tyburn (which may very probably be the case) than forfeit our integrity, or shock the faith of our reader." Here the ancients had a great advantage over the moderns, for Homer could always use Greek deities to deliver his characters, and the Arabians and Persians could use genii and fairies. Their intervention seemed probable to ancient readers, but moderns are confined to natural means alone.

Again Fielding shows us that the rules he establishes are not merely theoretical, but are laid down as a practical basis for his art. The rules of credibility are carefully followed throughout the novels.

The last introductory chapter, Book XVIII, Chapter I, A Farewell to the Reader, resumes the figure of the stage-coach journey, which Fielding has used in *Joseph Andrews*. The author and his readers, as fellow-travelers in a stage-coach, are now arrived at the last stage of their long journey. Like such fellow-travelers, "who, notwithstanding any bickerings or little animosities which may have occurred on the road, generally make all up at last, and mount, for the last time, into their vehicle with cheerfulness and good humour," he wishes that he and his readers may part friends. Just as "all jokes and raillery are at this time laid aside," and "the conversation is usually plain and serious," so in this last book he will abandon all his pleasantry and ludicrous observations and write plain, serious narrative. The variety of matter which he will be obliged "to cram into this book" leaves him no room for humorous comment.

Finally he wishes his reader well, saying, "If I have been an entertaining companion to thee it is what I have desired. If in anything I have offended, it was really without any intention." He seems anxious here, as earlier, to avoid any imputation of libel. He apprehends that the reader has been warned that he was "to travel with a very scurrilous fellow," but insists that "whoever told thee so did me an injury. . . No man detests and despises scurrility more than myself; nor hath any man more reason; for none hath ever been treated with more."

The reasons for this sensitiveness we have earlier indicated. His kindly farewell to the reader is characteristic. Not aloof from his readers like Hardy and Conrad, he is their friendly companion, traveling with them on their journey through his land of story, commenting upon his characters and chatting with his readers. His hope that he has been an entertaining companion is a final statement of his purpose to entertain and to interest his readers. Instruction is to be given only through these means. This has become the traditional purpose of the English novel since Fielding. The purpose of instruction in conduct had been considerably more important in Defoe and Richardson, both anxious to convey the middle-class doctrine of prudence and industry. Fielding turned in his two earlier novels to the purpose of entertainment because of his desire to tell a good story, rather than to teach rules of conduct. We may discern here the influence of the picaresque novel, the burlesque romance, and the comedy of manners, all of which aimed primarily to entertain.

Amelia contains little of significance to Fielding's theory of the novel. He omits here the introductory essay chapters and concentrates upon his story, making almost no comment upon his art. The only critical theorizing in the novel is in Book I, Chapter I, Containing the Exordium, etc. Here he states his subject as "the various accidents which befel a very worthy couple after their uniting in the state of matrimony." The value of such a history as this he conceives to be that it furnishes a model of human life, and considering life as an art to be learned and practiced by all, we may be instructed by this history "by observing minutely the several incidents which tend to the catastrophe or completion of the whole, and the minute causes whence those incidents are produced."

The dedication, addressed to "Ralph Allen, Esq.," emphasizes the moral purpose of the novel. "The following book is sincerely designed to promote the cause of virtue, and to expose some of the most glaring evils, as well public as private, which at present infest the country; though there is scarce, as I remember, a single stroke of satire aimed at any one person throughout the whole." He does not wish to take the time to theorize, for he says:

> I will not trouble you with a preface concerning the work, nor endeavour to obviate any criticisms which can be made on it. The good-natured reader, if his heart should be here affected, will be

inclined to pardon many faults for the pleasure he will receive from a tender sensation: and for readers of a different stamp, the more faults they can discover, the more, I am convinced, they will be pleased.

Fielding's purpose in *Amelia* is primarily didactic, which would obviously make artistic theorizing less appropriate. He had already stated his theory of the novel completely in the earlier novels, and is principally concerned here in promoting the cause of virtue and exposing glaring evils, such as gambling, dueling, crime in London, and the spunging-house. His work as justice of the peace on the Bow Street bench had given him a reformatory bent, which in *Amelia* assumes preeminence over his artistic purpose. No longer so keenly interested in the new literary form he is creating, he forsakes his comic attitude for the gravity of the reformer.

IV

FIELDING'S APPLICATION OF HIS THEORY

FIELDING consciously applied his theory of the novel as he wrote *Joseph Andrews* and *Tom Jones*. His theory, incomplete in *Joseph Andrews*, could not yet be fully applied; it remained for *Tom Jones* to exemplify it as a whole. When he wrote *Tom Jones*, his conception of the novel was complete. In *Joseph Andrews* his theory is stated only in broad outline, but insofar as stated it is practiced. In *Amelia* he seems to forget his comic theories and writes a sentimental novel which does not well exemplify his critical doctrines.

In defining his "comic romance" in the Author's Preface to *Joseph Andrews*, Fielding distinguishes it from comedy by its more extended and comprehensive action, its much larger circle of incidents, and its greater variety of characters. This is illustrated when we compare *Joseph Andrews* with any comedy of Fielding's day or of the Restoration. These comedies were limited by the exigencies of the stage to a few locations only. The number of scene divisions might be large, as in Congreve's *Way of the World*, but only a few settings were presented. Similarly, few incidents could occur within the limits of five acts and the few hours allowed for performance. The action of *Joseph Andrews* takes place in several dozens of locations, scattered along the road from London to Booby Hall, and covers all the significant actions of the characters over a period of from one to two weeks. It demonstrates the marked advantage of the novelist over the playwright in the extent and comprehensiveness of the action which he can present. That *Joseph Andrews* contains a larger circle of incidents and a greater variety of characters than a comedy follows logically. The average comedy of the period contains only about eight to a dozen characters, but few of which are important. In this number only a few variations in type were possible, and the formula of the comedy of manners tended to make the same types, such as the fop, the wit, the false wit, constantly recur. In *Joseph Andrews* we have dozens of characters of widely varying types, a few of which are the country clergyman, represented by Parsons Adams, Trulliber, and Barnabas, the great lady, Lady Booby, the lady's maid, Mrs. Slipslop, the innkeeper and his wife, Mr. and Mrs. Tow-wouse, the dishonest and ignorant lawyer, Lawyer Scout, the reformed rake, Mr. Wilson, the country squire, who is unnamed, and the ignorant country justice. No comedy had ever presented such great variety of characters. Fielding reveled in the scope for character portrayal which the novel afforded. He showed the possibilities of the novel in this respect better than any of his predecessors and clearly indicated the advantages of the novel over the comic drama.

The "comic romance," Fielding has told us, differs from the serious one in that its fable and action are light and ridiculous, its characters are sometimes of inferior rank and manners, and its sentiments and diction are ludicrous, burlesque sometimes being admitted in the diction. The fable of *Joseph Andrews* concerns the amusing adventures which befel Parson Adams, Joseph Andrews, Fanny, and their friends, as they journeyed along the road from London to their homes at and near Booby Hall. They meet with ridiculous mischances along the road and in their inns, they get into scrapes and out again, and always the comic point of view is sustained, the treatment is light and ridiculous. Joseph's virtuous resistance to the advances of Lady Booby is light ridicule of *Pamela*; his letters to his sister parody those of Pamela to her parents. The only exceptions to the light and ridiculous tone of the fable and action are *The History of Leonora, or The Unfortunate Jilt*, a bit of interpolated tragedy, and the story of Mr. Wilson, a serious moral tale. These digressions, which Fielding employs by the example of the classical epic and current fiction, mar the unity of the story and break its comic tone. They do, indeed, serve the purpose of contrast to the comic narrative and perhaps prevent the comic tone from becoming monotonous.

They might better have been omitted, however, in the interest of Fielding's art. We can reconcile them to his theory only by his rather doubtful rule that he may digress as often as he likes.

In *Joseph Andrews* characters of inferior rank and manners are numerous. Mrs. Slipslop, Lady Booby's maid, is a perfect example. She is ignorant, stupid, garrulous, prying, lascivious, bibulous, and ungrammatical, to name only a few of her traits which comprise "inferior manners." Mr. and Mrs. Tow-wouse, the avaricious and cynical innkeepers, and Betty, the chambermaid, with her stupid simplicity and naïve affection for Joseph, are other good specimens. The list includes more innkeepers, an hostler or two, a coachman, and various rustics. His portrayal of these "inferior" characters and their conversation shows Fielding's familiarity with the lower classes and their speech, which he insists is as important to the novelist as a knowledge of "upper life."

The sentiments and diction of *Joseph Andrews* are mainly ludicrous, and there is much burlesque diction. Fielding is careful to observe the distinction which he has made between burlesque in the sentiments and in the diction, the latter only being allowable in the comic romance, which is consequently not pure burlesque. Although he respects and admires the virtues of Parson Adams, he makes him a laughable figure. His feeling toward him and toward all his characters consists of mingled sympathy and amusement. He makes the unworldliness of Adams, his book-learning and ignorance of mankind, and even his kindness and honesty, the subject of gentle, sympathetic laughter. Similarly he makes Joseph's virtue amusing, and Lady Booby's amorousness ludicrous. Even when Joseph is stripped naked by thieves and left lying in a ditch, he makes his plight ludicrous, as he describes the rescue by the party in the stage-coach. Behind the ludicrousness of the sentiments and diction, of course, is Fielding's purpose, often accomplished by keen ironic satire, of laughing vice out of the world.

Burlesque diction, we were told, would sometimes occur in the description of the battles, and other places "not necessary to be pointed out to the classical reader." The best of the battle scenes is the one in Book III, Chapter VI, which describes in true Homeric style the encounter between Joseph and Parson Adams and the hunting dogs. A most amusing passage describes Joseph going to the rescue of Adams. The detailed description of Joseph's cudgel recalls that of the shield of Achilles in *The Iliad*. Similar burlesque battles appear in *The Battle of the Books*, *Hudibras*, and *The Dunciad*. Other Homeric burlesques in *Joseph Andrews* are the invocations to morning and evening in Book I, Chapter VIII, and the panegyrics to love and vanity in Book I, Chapter VII.

In this kind of writing, Fielding has told us, the author should confine himself strictly to nature, thus distinguishing the comic romance from pure burlesque and the romances. Fielding's realism is best witnessed by the praise of all his critics, for so accurately portraying eighteenth century England. Those who know most about the life of the times have praised him most highly for his keen observation of all kinds of life. Gibbon speaks of *Tom Jones* as an exquisite picture of manners, and similar tribute has been paid to *Joseph Andrews*. Its realism is neither so complete nor so convincing as that of *Tom Jones*, but it is accurate so far as it goes, giving us the best picture of life in England's rural inns until the publication of *Tom Jones*. Sir Walter Raleigh thinks one of Fielding's great contributions to the art of the novel is "a realism in the characters and events . . . convincing without hampering the freedom of the artist. . . It is not laborious and minute but it is sufficient. He does not, like Defoe, 'protest too much,' for his object is to create an illusion of reality and not a belief in fact. . . Fielding's acquaintance with life is fully as wide as Defoe's, while his insight is keener and deeper. . . Others before him had seen and known these things, but in Fielding's pages for the first time they are introduced with no loss of reality to subserve the ends of fiction. Common life is the material of the story [*Joseph Andrews*] but it is handled here for the first time with the freedom and imagination of a great artist."[1] Saintsbury gives similar tribute: "They all (the greater works), even the *Voyage*, hang to-

[1] W. Raleigh, *The English Novel*, p.177.

gether as being direct pictures of life." Defoe, he says, misses complete lifelikeness; *Pamela* brought the novel nearer reality, "but something was wanting; and this something Fielding gave in *Joseph Andrews*."[1] A single example of the realism of *Joseph Andrews* will suffice; Book I, Chapter XIV, Being Very Full of Adventures Which Succeeded Each Other at the Inn, vividly illustrates Fielding's concrete portrayal of low life, recalling the picaresque realism of *Gil Blas*.

Fielding's greatest skill, however, is not in creating background, but in portraying character. No discussion of his realism would be complete without mentioning Parson Adams, the greatest character he ever drew, and according to Scott, Coleridge, and Leigh Hunt, the greatest character in English fiction. Adams is best revealed by his speeches and actions, for Fielding portrays character dramatically. Book II, Chapter II, is a typical scene, revealing Adams's unworldliness and love of books, his amusing forgetfulness and absentmindedness.

Fielding's theory of satire is steadily applied in *Joseph Andrews*. The characters chiefly satirized are Lady Booby, Mrs. Slipslop, Peter Pounce, Mr. Barnabas, Parson Trulliber, Mrs. Tow-wouse, the group in the stage-coach, and Pamela Andrews, who appears at the end of the novel. Lady Booby's affectation of virtue and refinement is consistently ridiculed. She is shown to be as "low," in her uncontrollable longing for Joseph and in all her genuine emotions, as her crude and hideous maid, Mrs. Slipslop. Mrs. Slipslop is also a hypocrite, like her mistress, affecting virtue. Fielding's ridicule of both characters is best seen in Book I, Chapter VII, where they confer about Joseph, both professing abhorrence for him, but revealing secret affection.

Peter Pounce, Lady Booby's steward, is satirized for his affectation of honesty and generosity, to conceal unscrupulous greed. He, "on urgent occasions, used to advance the servants their wages: not before they were due, but before they were payable; that is, perhaps, half a year after they were due; and this at the moderate premium of fifty per cent or a little more: by which

[1] G. Saintsbury, Introduction to *Fielding*, in the *Masters of English Literature* Series.

charitable methods, together with lending money to other people, and even to his own master and mistress, the honest man had, from nothing, in a few years amassed a small sum of twenty thousand pounds or thereabouts." He recalls Molière's Harpagon, with whom Fielding was familiar through his adaptation of *L'Avare*. Fielding's irony, the chief weapon of his satire, is admirably illustrated in this passage.

Mr. Barnabas and Parson Trulliber, both hypocritical clergymen, are foils to Adams. Mr. Barnabas affects piety to conceal unscrupulous selfishness and vanity. The latter he displays when Joseph is brought to the Tow-wouses' inn after being robbed. He shows great zeal in the business, though he has no interest in it other than "to display his parts" in upholding public justice This gives Fielding the occasion for a "sarcastical panegyric" on vanity, very like those in *Vanity Fair*. Barnabas's affected piety appears when he reproves the surgeon, in Book II, Chapter XVI, for speaking disrespectfully of Tillotson's sermons, and then advises Adams to misrepresent his sermons as those "of a clergyman lately deceased" in order "to make some money of them." He tells Adams he is to receive double price for preaching a eulogistic funeral sermon upon a magistrate known to be immoral and vicious. Trulliber is satirized for his greed, selfishness, and coarseness, when Adams goes to him to borrow a little money. He pretends pious friendship for his brother clergyman, until he discovers that Adams wants a loan, when he turns upon Adams angrily and orders him from the house. He shows his coarseness by the crude joke he plays upon Adams, sending him into the pigsty, where he falls flat in the filth. Barnabas and Trulliber show us the eighteenth century church at its worst; Adams, at its best.

Mrs. Tow-wouse conceals, none too well, a hard mercenary spirit beneath an affectation of Christian charity. When Joseph is first brought wounded to her inn, and she thinks him penniless, she says to her henpecked husband, "Where's his money to pay his reckoning? Why doth not such a fellow go to an alehouse? I shall send him packing as soon as I am up, I assure you" . . .

"My dear," said he, "common charity won't suffer you to do that." "Common charity teaches us to provide for ourselves and our families," said she, "and I and mine won't be ruined by your charity, I assure you." Later, when she suspects Joseph to be a gentleman of some importance, she says, "God forbid she should not discharge the duty of a Christian, since the poor gentleman was brought to her house. She had a natural antipathy to vagabonds; but could pity the misfortunes of a Christian as soon as another."

The group of characters in the stage-coach which passes the spot where Joseph lies naked and wounded is satirized for callous selfishness disguised under affectations of prudence and delicacy. The incident is a general indictment of the selfishness of average mankind and has a touch of grim irony about it which indicates the serious moral purpose behind Fielding's satire. The generosity of the lowly postillion is beautiful beside the selfishness of the passengers.

Pamela is satirized toward the close of the story. Now that she has raised her family by marrying Mr. B., she admonishes Joseph not to debase it by marrying Fanny. She conceals the snobbish pride of the parvenu beneath an affected gratitude and sense of duty. "Brother," said she, "Mr. Booby advises you as a friend; and no doubt my papa and mama will be of his opinion, and will have great reason to be angry with you for destroying what his goodness hath done, and throwing down our family again, after he hath raised it. It would become you better, brother, to pray for the assistance of grace against such a passion than to indulge it. . . I hope I shall never behave with an unbecoming pride: but, at the same time, I shall always endeavour to know myself, and question not the assistance of grace to that purpose." Fielding here shows Richardson's character in her true colors, as a selfish little hypocrite.

The purpose of instruction by presenting good examples of human character is carried out in Adams, Joseph, Fanny, and Mr. Wilson in his reformed state. Among them they possess all the traits which Fielding considers the highest human virtues.

Adams has generosity, kindness, honesty, idealism, and a truly Christian attitude toward life. In spite of his eccentricities and laughableness, he embodies the highest spiritual virtues. Fielding, like his readers, loves this character. He is thought to have patterned him after his friend the Rev. Mr. Young, and perhaps his friends Ralph Allen and Lord Lyttleton. Joseph, barring the prudishness which Fielding was forced by his parody of *Pamela* to give him, has beauty, courage, honesty, generosity, and nearly the whole catalogue of manly virtues. He lacks only the mellow wisdom and sweetness which Adams's religion and reading have given him. Fanny is the feminine counterpart of Joseph, with all the sweet womanly virtues, beauty, chastity, modesty, tenderness, and loyalty. In these two characters Fielding comes close to violating his rule of not presenting perfectly good characters. Mr. Wilson, though formerly a rake, has accomplished a perfect reformation and lives the eighteenth century conception of the philosophic life in the peaceful, beautiful English countryside with his wife and children, doing a little farming and gardening, like Horace, studying, and disporting himself with his family. Such a life, one thinks, Fielding would have liked to live, away from the bustle and sick hurry of London.

Tom Jones fully exemplifies Fielding's theory of the novel. To *Tom Jones* the "comic romance" theory applies as well as to *Joseph Andrews*. In addition, the rules introduced in *Tom Jones* are put in practice. Like the earlier novel it contains all the elements of the epic except numbers and differs from comedy as the serious epic differs from tragedy. The action covers the youth of its hero, from his birth until he is about twenty-one years of age, dealing with dozens of significant episodes during that period, comprehending everything of importance to the portrayal of Tom's character. This comedy could not do. Forty-four characters, at least twenty of whom are important to the story, appear in *Tom Jones*, in even greater variety than in *Joseph Andrews*. The fable and action are "light and ridiculous" in lesser degree than in *Joseph Andrews*, containing more of the "grave and solemn." The prevailing tone is still comic, however, and there is much ridicule of affectation. More instruction is to be found here than in *Joseph Andrews*. Allworthy, for example, personifies almost perfect goodness, and Blifil is the very type of wicked hypocrisy. Moral comment is also more frequent and lengthy. Persons of inferior rank and manners are introduced, foremost among whom are Partridge, Mrs. Honour, Black George, and Deborah Wilkins, followed by the numerous innkeepers, hostlers, barmaids, and chambermaids who crowd the pages of the novel. The sentiments and diction are mainly ludicrous, burlesque diction sometimes being used. Tom's adventures are usually treated in the comic vein. Though sometimes serious in intent, Fielding seldom forsakes his playful manner.

Burlesque diction occurs in Book II, Chapter IV, in the mock-heroic battle between Mr. and Mrs. Partridge, and in Book IV, Chapter II, in a description of Sophia Western in the mock-sublime classical style. Another Homeric battle, between Molly Seagrim and the parish, appears in Book IV, Chapter VIII. In Book IX, Chapter III, Susan, the chambermaid, does battle better than Thalestris the Amazon, and in Chapter V Jones outdoes Ulysses at table and engages with Mrs. Waters in a burlesque battle of love.

Tom Jones never sinks into pure burlesque, strictly confining itself to nature. True to the promise of Book I, Chapter I, it shows us as much of the "prodigious variety" of life as it is possible for an author to deal with. The wonderful originality of *Tom Jones*, the characters and plot being taken from his own knowledge and experience, shows the maturity of Fielding's powers as a realist. *Joseph Andrews* owed a direct debt to other novelists, but in *Tom Jones* this debt is negligible. It is the most complete and realistic picture of life in mid-eighteenth century England.

In *Tom Jones* Fielding's theory of satire is again practiced. We must modify, however, the statement that "the ridiculous only . . . falls within my province," because of the more frequent serious passages. The rest of the theory applies completely. Affectation, springing from vanity or hypocrisy, is ridiculed in many characters, most bitterly in the villain of the novel, Blifil, who has all the traits Fielding most deeply despises. The author's hatred of this character occasionally destroys his customary self-control and humorous restraint, and he breaks forth into bitter irony against so despicable a person. Blifil is the worst sort of hypocrite, who affects Christian virtue to conceal selfish and unscrupulous ambition and malicious scheming. Outwardly all benevolence, piety, and prudence, he is clever enough to deceive even Allworthy, his patron. He is used constantly as a foil to Tom's manly honesty and good-nature.

The only satire directed against Allworthy is gentle ridicule of the too trusting nature through which he is deceived by Blifil. Thwackum and Square, the hypocritical divine and the philosopher, affect piety and wisdom, respectively, as cloaks for selfishness and greed. Fielding points the contrast between their pious and wise speech and their selfish and vicious conduct. Bridget Allworthy and Deborah Wilkins affect virtue, the former to conceal immoral conduct, the latter, cruel selfishness. Mrs. Western is ridiculed for affected learning, springing from vanity rather than from hypocrisy. In order to impress people with her learning she affects merely greater knowledge of life and politics than she actually possesses. Mrs. Honour similarly affects a higher degree of refinement and virtue than she really has. Molly Seagrim, however, pretends to a virtue which she does not at all possess, as do Mrs. Waters and Lady Bellaston. Partridge, out of vanity, professes much more than his share of learning; Lord Fellamar, a hypocrite, shows a sense of honor and courtesy merely outward. Ensign Northerton hypocritically affects soldierly courage, and Mrs. Fitzpatrick, womanly virtue. The only characters completely without affectation are Tom, Sophia, Squire Western, and Allworthy. Fielding's deliberate satire is never directed toward them, though he makes good-natured fun of them. The hypocrites he ridicules severely, often with bitter irony; the vain he makes merely laughable. He never satirizes vice, deformity, or calamity unless they are touched with affectation.

Book I, Chapter I, of *Tom Jones* announces that Fielding will serve to his readers the fare of human nature, first in the plain simplicity of country life, and later in the vice and affectation of city life. He provides this fare by setting his scene first at the country seat of Squire Allworthy and depicting the life surrounding it, introducing such rustic characters as Black George and Partridge, with the village groups as a background. The scene shifts later to the road to London, on which Tom sets out after his exile from Allworthy's, and along which Sophia flees from her father's attempt to marry her to Blifil. They at last reach London, where we find the vice and affectation of city life represented in Lady Bellaston and Lord Fellamar, with whom, respectively, our hero and heroine become involved. That Fielding's fare is true human nature during both the country and the city phases of the story is testified by the unanimous praise which has always been given to their realism. Fielding had lived in the country at East Stour, in London for many years, and had often traveled the roads to London. He was thus closely acquainted with these backgrounds and with the types of people to be found in each.

In Book II, Chapter I, Fielding says he will use the selective historical method, describing only significant events in the lives of his characters, skipping over periods when nothing important happened. In practice he skips several such periods, the time covered in his books and chapters varying widely. Book II covers two years; twelve years are omitted between Books II and III; three years are covered in Book III, one in Book IV. Later, when the plot is nearing its climax, we find Book VIII containing about two days, and Book IX, twelve hours. The actions of the characters are always treated at a length befitting their importance, and not according to the time elapsing or the number of events.

In *Tom Jones* we find many delightful instances, some serious and some burlesque, of poetic ornament, which Fielding told us would distinguish his novel from pure history. The best of the serious poetic passages is the introduction of Sophia in Book IV, Chapter II, inspired by Fielding's love for his wife. Several of the burlesque passages, the mock-heroic battles, have already been pointed out. A burlesque classical simile appears in Book I, Chapter VI, where Mrs. Deborah is Introduced into the Parish with a Simile, and a burlesque description of the coming of morning occurs in Book IX, Chapter IX. Other poetic passages are scattered at intervals throughout the novel.

Fielding preserves in his story the balanced, tolerant attitude toward his characters described in Book VII, Chapter I, never condemning them for single acts, but examining their motives and the general tenor of their lives. Blifil is the only person of whom he is intolerant, and we can forgive him that; for Blifil's consistently selfish motives and hypocritical actions would make him intolerable to an angel. But if a character has the slightest tincture of good, Fielding will not condemn it. Tom is forgiven his sins because of his fundamental goodness of heart. The sneaking dishonesty of Partridge is overlooked because he sometimes shows sincerity and generosity. Black George is forgiven his dishonesty because of occasional kindness and gratitude. Fielding shows us that the essentially good are capable of bad or unjust actions; witness Tom's affairs with Molly Seagrim, Mrs. Waters, and Lady Bellaston. Allworthy is guilty of unjust anger against Tom; otherwise his motives and character are well-nigh perfect. The gist of Fielding's wisdom in judging his characters is in examining motives and fundamental traits, pronouncing final judgment only upon these. With rare tolerance, he can condemn an act without condemning the person who performs it.

In *Tom Jones* Fielding adheres closely to the rules of credibility. There is nothing supernatural in the novel. Although Ensign Northerton thought he saw a ghost when Tom appeared, looking ghostly enough, the reader well knows he did not. Every incident in the story is real and probable. Some critics have objected to the excessive use of coincidence, the way in which characters meet or miss one another or money is lost or found to suit the needs of the plot. The test of coincidence in fiction is whether or not it seems probable, as it does in *Tom Jones*. As Hardy has shown in *The Return of the Native* and *Tess of the D'Urbervilles*, its use is perfectly legitimate so long as it has this air of credibility about it.

Allworthy and Blifil are the only improbable characters in *Tom Jones*. Allworthy is a model of passionless perfection, an ideal rather than a real character. He would be more probable if he had some frailty or idiosyncrasy other than the lack of insight which makes him trust Blifil. Blifil is too wicked to be probable; there is a lack of reality in his precocity and his schemes to further his own interests. Fielding was obviously obsessed with hatred of his hypocrisy.

All the other characters are fully credible. Although he admires Tom and wants his readers to admire his hero, Fielding is more careful to make him real and probable than to make him admirable. Tom has much about him which is attractive; he is handsome, generous, and good-humored. But the blemishes in his character caused by his excess of youthful passion make many admirers of the novel object to its hero and to Fielding's tolerance for his blemishes. He is more real because of them, however. Fielding says in Book X, Chapter I, that no good purpose is served by introducing characters of angelic perfection or diabolical depravity. Although inconsistent with this opinion in drawing Allworthy and Blifil, he proves its soundness in the character of Tom, who, with all his shortcomings, appeals very strongly to our sympathies and teaches us to shun his faults. The teaching is the more effective, as Fielding said, because we like and sympathize with Tom.

Squire Western is the most vivid portrait of the country squire that exists. In spite of his grotesqueness and marked idiosyncrasies, probably no one has ever said he is a caricature. In this character Fielding demonstrates what delightful effects can be gained by introducing the surprising and unusual while still clinging to credibility. Some have objected to Squire Western's cowardice when struck by Lord Fellamar's friend as inconsistent and not in character; but considering that the squire is a country fellow in London, being bluffed by a city fellow, this cowardice seems natural and not a great stain on his courage.

The reality and beauty of Sophia Western's character is witnessed by the opinion of many critics. She takes a very high position among the finest women portrayed by the dramatist and novelist. Schiller thought Shakespeare's Juliet and Fielding's Sophia superior to the most beautiful feminine portraits of antiquity.[1] Mrs. Barbauld, while thinking Sophia too indelicate, nevertheless admired her.[2] Thackeray liked her and expressed compassion for her as a "fond, foolish, palpitating little creature." Nearly all critics have joined in praising her reality.

The qualities essential to the novelist, stated in Book IX, Chapter I, Fielding himself possessed in a high degree. His genius has been acknowledged to be largely responsible for the development of the modern novel. His understanding and keen observation of life and his portrayal of it in *Joseph Andrews* and *Tom Jones* laid the basis for the realistic novel of our day. His learning appears in his wide acquaintance with ancient and modern writers. The many vivid scenes in drawing-rooms and inns in his novels give abundant evidence of his experience in both high and low life. His sensitiveness and sympathy are seen in his portrayal of human passion, as in the love scenes of Tom and Sophia. He shares the feelings of his characters as he creates them, so that they become living beings in his hands. Ernest A. Baker calls Fielding's art "intellectual realism."[3] Since Fielding, he believes, this method, by which the author conceives of his characters intellectually and gives them imaginative reality, has prevailed in English fiction.

Fielding's theory of the novel is important as the first explicit formula for the English novel. All succeeding theorists have necessarily, though perhaps unconsciously, built upon the foundation which he laid. Though he made little effort to organize his rules into a complete code, they state all the essentials of the modern novel and constitute a sound and coherent body of doctrine.

[1] *Briefe*, ed. Fritz Jonas, vol. IV, p.355.
[2] *British Novelists*, vol. XVIII, Preface, p.xiv.
[3] *The History of the English Novel*, vol. IV, Preface, p.5.

BIBLIOGRAPHY

ARISTOTLE, *The Poetics*, trans. Lane Cooper. New York, Ginn, 1913.

BAKER, ERNEST A., *The History of the English Novel*, vol. IV. London, Witherby, 1930.

BALDWIN, EDWARD C., *The Character Books of the Seventeenth Century, in Relation to the Development of the Novel*, in *The Western Reserve University Bulletin*, October, 1900.

BANERJI, HIRAN K., *Henry Fielding, Playwright, Journalist, and Master of the Art of Fiction: His Life and Works*. Oxford, Blackwell, 1929.

BLANCHARD, FREDERIC T., *Fielding the Novelist: a Study in Historical Criticism*. New Haven, Yale University Press, 1926.

BURTON, RICHARD, *Masters of the English Novel*. New York, Holt, 1909.

BUTLER, SAMUEL, *Hudibras*, Bohn Library. London, Bell, 1859.

CERVANTES, MIGUEL, *Don Quixote*, Everyman's Library. London, Dent, 1909.

CHANDLER, FRANK W., *The Literature of Roguery*. Boston, Houghton, Mifflin & Co., 1907.

CONGREVE, WILLIAM, *The Way of the World*, in *Restoration Plays from Dryden to Farquhar*, Everyman's Library. London, Dent, 1905.

CROSS, WILBUR L., *The Development of the English Novel*. New York, Macmillan, 1899.

——— *The History of Henry Fielding*. New Haven, Yale University Press, 1918.

DAWSON, WILLIAM J., *The Makers of English Fiction*. New York, Revell, 1905.

DEFOE, DANIEL, *Robinson Crusoe, Moll Flanders*, in *Works*, Bohn Library. London, Bell, 1882.

DIGEON, AURÉLIEN, *Les Romans de Fielding*. Paris, 1923. English translation, London, Routledge, 1925.

DOBRÉE, BONAMY, *Restoration Comedy, 1660-1720*. Oxford, Clarendon Press, 1924.

DOBSON, AUSTIN, *Fielding*, in *English Men of Letters*. New York, Harper, 1883.

—— —— Fielding's Library, in *Eighteenth Century Vignettes*. London, Chatto and Windus, 1892.

ELWIN, WHITWELL, Fielding in *The Quarterly Review*, Dec., 1855, vol. XCVIII, no. CXCV, pp.100–148; reprinted in his *Some XVIII Men of Letters*. London, Murray, 1902.

FIELDING, HENRY, *Works*, edited with an Introduction, by George Saintsbury, 12 vols. London, Dent, 1893.

—— —— *Works*, edited with an Introduction, by William E. Henley. New York, Croscup and Sterling, 1902.

—— —— *Joseph Andrews*, ed. J. B. Priestley. London, Lane, 1929.

FIELDING, SARAH, *The Adventures of David Simple*. London, 1744.

FURETIÈRE, ANTOINE, *Le Roman Bourgeois*, ed. Fournier. Paris, Jannet, 1854.

GODDEN, GRACE M., *Henry Fielding: a Memoir*. London, Sampson Low, Marston, 1910.

HAZLITT, WILLIAM, *Lectures on the English Comic Writers*. London, 1819. London, Dent, 1903.

HOMER, *The Iliad*, trans. Lang, Leaf, and Myers. London, Macmillan, 1883.

—— *The Odyssey*, trans. Butcher and Lang. London, 1879. New York, Modern Library, 1929.

HORACE, *Ars Poetica*, trans. Roscommon. London, 1709.

LAWRENCE, FREDERICK, *Life of Henry Fielding*. London, Hall, Virtue, 1855.

LESAGE, ALAIN R., *Gil Blas*, trans. Smollett, Bohn Library. London, Bell, 1900.

LONGINUS, *On the Sublime*, trans. Spurdens. London, 1836.

MARIVAUX, PIERRE, *Le Paysan Parvenu*, *Marianne*, in *Oeuvres*, ed. Duviquet. Paris, 1825.

MEREDITH, GEORGE, *An Essay on Comedy*, ed. Lane Cooper. New York, Scribner, 1918.

MOLIÈRE, JEAN B. P., *L'Avare*, *Le Bourgeois Gentilhomme*, in *Oeuvres Complètes*, ed. Moland. Paris, Gurnier, 1863-64.

PALMER, JOHN L., *The Comedy of Manners*. London, Bell, 1913.

PLATO, *Ion*, *Phaedrus*, trans. Benjamin Jowett. New York, Oxford University Press, 1892.

POPE, ALEXANDER, *Memoirs of the Life, Works, and Discoveries of Martinus Scriblerus*, Book II, The Bathos, or the Art of Sinking in Poetry; *The Dunciad*; *An Essay on Criticism*; in *Works*, ed. Elwin and Courthope. London, Murray, 1871-89.

PRÉVOST, ANTOINE F., *Manon Lescaut*. London, 1841.

RALEIGH, SIR WALTER, *The English Novel*. New York, Scribner, 1894.

RICHARDSON, SAMUEL, *Pamela*, *Clarissa Harlowe*, in *Works*, ed. L. Stephen. London, Sotheran, 1883.

SAINTSBURY, GEORGE, *The History of the French Novel*. London, Macmillan, 1917-19.

—— —— Introduction to *Masters of English Literature: Fielding*. London, Bell, 1909.

SCARRON, PAUL, *Le Roman Comique*, ed. Fournel. Paris, Plon, 1857.

SMITH, DAVID NICHOL, Johnson and Boswell, in *The Cambridge History of English Literature*, vol. x. Cambridge, England, University Press, 1913.

SMOLLETT, TOBIAS, *Roderick Random*, *Humphrey Clinker*, in *Works*, ed. George Saintsbury. London, Gibbings, 1900-03.

SPINGARN, JOEL E., *The History of Literary Criticism in the Renaissance*, Columbia University *Studies in Literature*. New York, Macmillan, 1899.

STEPHEN, SIR LESLIE, Fielding's Novels, in *Hours in a Library, Third Series*. London, Smith, Elder, 1892.

STERNE, LAURENCE, *Tristram Shandy*, Everyman's Library. London, Dent, n.d.

——— *A Sentimental Journey*, Everyman's Library. London, Dent, 1926.

THACKERAY, WILLIAM M., *Vanity Fair*. London, 1848. Everyman's Library, London, Dent, 1922.

——— *English Humourists of the Eighteenth Century*. New York, Harper, 1853.

THOMSON, CLARA L., *Samuel Richardson: a Biographical and Critical Study*. London, Marshall, 1900.

THORNBURY, ETHEL M., *Fielding and the Comic Prose Epic*, University of Wisconsin *Studies in Language and Literature*, No. 30. Madison, 1931.

THORNDIKE, ASHLEY H., *English Comedy*. New York, Macmillan, 1929.

TRAILL, HENRY D., *Sterne*, in *English Men of Letters*. London, Macmillan, 1882.

VANBRUGH, SIR JOHN, *The Provoked Wife*, in *Restoration Drama from Dryden to Farquhar*, Everyman's Library. London, Dent, 1905.

WYCHERLEY, WILLIAM, *The Country Wife*, in *Restoration Drama from Dryden to Farquhar*, Everyman's Library. London, Dent, 1905.

INDEX